"This book has the potential to offer people so much hope, as well as guidance for living with more inner peace about both life and death."
—César Valdez, LMSW, Co-Executive Director of IADC

"Dr. Tom Nehmy has created something truly extraordinary. *Inspired Life, Beautiful Death* is a profound and deeply moving exploration of grief, healing, and the nature of our eternal existence. With wisdom, compassion, and groundbreaking insights, Tom reveals how love never dies—and neither do we. This book is a gift to anyone seeking comfort, clarity, and a renewed connection to the ones they love beyond this life."
—Sandra Champlain, #1 international bestselling author of *We Don't Die: A Skeptic's Discovery of Life After Death* and host of *We Don't Die Radio* & *Shades of the Afterlife*

"In this wonderful book, Dr Nehmy, a dedicated researcher, has explored the power of a new and very effective therapeutic method – Induced After-Death Communication (IADC) - for people who are living with unresolved grief, loss and sadness. He provides descriptive accounts of his meticulous research and the amazing results it provides. It is a riveting book, beautifully written, fully accessible, and a must-read for anybody in grief or who works with those who are grieving.

Dr Nehmy also opens the reader to new perspectives for living a more meaningful life, reducing the fear of death, and looking forward to reunion with loved ones."
—Elizabeth Keane MSW, PhD, author of *Amazing Encounters*

"This book is a compelling read! The author leaves the reader in no doubt about the existence of life after death and how the powerful therapy of IADC in compassionate hands can facilitate a connectedness between worlds. The reader is taken on a journey which includes personal stories and beliefs, scientific knowledge, and heart-felt case histories resulting in the heaviness of grief being replaced with a new and lighter life-affirming energy."

—Joy Nugent OAM, palliative care pioneer and founder of Soul Talks Inc.

"Grief is an unwelcome visitor we all eventually meet. In *Inspired Life, Beautiful Death*, Dr. Tom Nehmy doesn't just meet grief—he wrestles it to the ground, questioning everything he thought he knew about the limits of human healing. The result is an eye-opening investigation into *Induced After-Death Communication* (IADC) Therapy, a radical method that bridges the gap between science and spirituality.

What elevates this book is the author's own vulnerability and willingness to question everything, including himself, making his discoveries all the more powerful—and all the more credible. Dr. Nehmy invites readers into a world where grief, when faced head-on, can lead to profound healing and reconnection. For those willing to take the journey, the reward is not just a better understanding of loss, but a deeper appreciation of life.

A wonderful piece of work—thank you, Dr. Nehmy."

—Stephen Berkley, filmmaker and director of the multi-award-winning feature documentary *Life with Ghosts*

"This book combines the rigour of the scientific method with deep empathy for the human experience of loss and grief to present us with compelling data in support of consciousness's survival of death and a vision of life in which love, connection and purpose transcend our singular existence.

In documenting the IADC method Dr Nehmy not only demonstrates a powerful methodology to alleviate individual suffering, he also opens a door for us all to understand the implications of the fact that death is not the end."

—Kim McCaul, author of *Multidimensional Evolution: Personal explorations of consciousness*

Inspired Life, Beautiful Death

Tom Nehmy, PhD

FORMIDABLE
PRESS

Formidable Press
www.formidablepress.com

ISBN (Hardcover): 978-0-6485004-5-2
ISBN (Paperback): 978-0-6485004-4-5
ISBN (eBook): 978-0-6485004-3-8
ISBN (Audiobook): 978-0-6485004-6-9

Legal Notice

Cover design by ebooklaunch.com
Interior design by Polgarus Studio

Also by Dr Tom Nehmy

Apples for the Mind
Creating emotional balance, peak performance & lifelong wellbeing

To Jasper

There is no death.
There are no limits.
All things are possible.

Contents

Foreword by Dr Allan Botkin

More than 25 years ago, I discovered a remarkable grief therapy by accident. As an early adopter of the trauma therapy known as EMDR, I started tweaking the standard protocol trying to improve its effectiveness. Some of the changes resulted in additional benefits to my patients, but nothing prepared me for the day a patient reported an after-death communication (ADC) – a powerful sense of reconnection with his deceased loved one – healing to a degree I had thought was not possible.

This singular event changed the trajectory of my professional life. As I began to explore and refine what would become Induced After-Death Communication (IADC) therapy, I witnessed hundreds of similar outcomes. Combat veterans, bereaved parents, and individuals from all walks of life were finding healing through these remarkable experiences. What started as an accidental discovery evolved into a structured therapeutic approach that consistently helps people transform their grief.

Dr. Tom Nehmy's *Inspired Life, Beautiful Death* is a must-read for both professional grief therapists and people who have lost a loved one. In his book he describes his research using IADC therapy, still a relatively new technique in psychotherapy terms, to treat grief in two 90-minute sessions. His client outcomes are consistently healing and uplifting.

Dr. Nehmy's work also offers profound insights into life and death.

His conclusions provide all of us a sense of comfort, along with a decrease in our fear of death, and a decrease in our deep suffering that accompanies the death of a loved one.

As the originator of IADC therapy, I have trained a few hundred therapists in this new method. There are now IADC therapists all over the world. While I am now retired, I see Dr. Nehmy as a rising superstar among our international IADC team. He is an outstanding clinician, and a dedicated scientifically minded researcher.

IADC is here to stay simply because it works. It has recently experienced accelerated growth worldwide because formal research studies are now supporting hundreds of prior clinical reports. I have said all along that the only problem with IADC is that it sounds too good to be true. I urge you to take a look. You won't be disappointed.

—Allan L. Botkin, Psy.D.

Discoverer and Founder of IADC
Author of *Induced After Death Communication: A Miraculous Therapy for Grief and Loss*

Chapter 1

The Beginning

Sobs wracked the young man's body as he sat on my therapists' couch, describing the death of his young wife, just two weeks before. A carefree boat trip and reef tour on their honeymoon had somehow resulted in her lifeless body being retrieved from the water. I didn't pry into details about the cause of death because I had an immediate problem I was expected to address: my client was devastated, I was his therapist, it was my job to help him.

"I'm so sorry," was my lame but heartfelt response when the young man described his confusion and despair at his young wife not returning to the boat.

"Everyone's sorry," he groaned as he sunk back into the couch, eyes desperate beneath his tortured brow, searching for a sign of hope that I'd be able provide more than just my sympathy.

Try as I might, I couldn't hide a deep helplessness that had entrenched itself within me when working with grieving people. My impotence stemmed from an apparently obvious realisation: I couldn't fix their problem. Bring me all your anxiety disorders, your depression, your child behaviour problems, your every other conceivable issue, and I at least have a fighting chance. But with grief, it feels like all I can do is stand beside them, staring into the abyss.

No amount of cognitive restructuring, behaviour diaries, empathy, or supportive counselling was going to make a substantive difference for these clients. Sure, I could sit with them in their distress, I could guide them to self-care, I could help them feel less alone. But I couldn't bring them back to their prior state of health, to make them whole again. And I sure as hell couldn't reestablish the loving connection they'd had stripped away.

I'm also still haunted by the tall, uptight, heavy-set lady in her thirties with hair pulled back so tight I wondered if her scalp hurt, whose chest heaved with each asthmatic breath as she recounted her father's sudden death by heart attack. One minute her life was whole and she was content, another it felt like the foundations of her life had been stripped from beneath her. She, too, needed more from me when her family doctor referred her for help with stress, anxiety, and grief.

The hope and confidence I had seen in her eyes in the first two sessions, as I listened so earnestly and validated her pain, slowly drained, as she realised there was nothing I could or would do that was going to significantly ease her pain. Or help her return to work and carry on with the day-to-day functioning that her young family needed from her.

I *desperately* wanted to help this lady. I mean, I wanted to help all my clients, but this lady was so... reasonable, so fundamentally human in her simple loves and needs. I felt that lump in my throat I'd sometimes get when I let myself get lost in a client's story. She loved her kids, loved her husband, and was doing her level best to live, work, and express her love.

She so loved her dad, too. Then he died.

I pulled my emotions back.

Didn't I have any *tools*? Clients want *tools* to manage their emotions and I'm supposed to have therapeutic *tools* with which to help them. Where were my fucking tools?

She eventually realised I was well-intentioned but ultimately useless and didn't come back. From there, my helplessness in the face of grief only grew. Despite my best efforts and intentions, I knew I was falling short in providing the support and healing my grieving clients so desperately needed. I couldn't shake the sense that there had to be a better way, a more effective approach to help them heal their pain, find peace, and reclaim their lives.

Chapter 2

An Amazing Therapy

Today, I fantasise about calling that bereft lady and young man back. I want to tell them I can help them now. What changed? I found a therapy that works.

Induced After-Death Communication (IADC) Therapy can, in two ninety-minute sessions, dramatically reduce a grieving client's sadness and even help them perceive the presence of the deceased person. I know, it sounds crazy, right? And surely too good to be true. Trust me, I've brought my sceptical scientific lens to this, and I'm still here. It's extremely effective at reducing sadness, and the reported spiritual phenomena – the part that gets a bit awkward for professionals like me – is as fascinating and healing as it sounds. In fact, I'm so convinced of the potential for this marriage of psychology and spirituality to help the world, I've undertaken a university-approved research project to assess it in a scientific and clinical way. I asked nine of my project's 43 participants if they'd be willing for me to share their stories in this book. All nine immediately said yes. Like me, they want the world to know it's possible to dramatically reduce the sadness associated with grief. Many of them have described their experience as life-changing. And like so many amazing things, it was discovered by accident. But before I tell you how IADC was discovered, you need to know about the therapy it evolved from: a therapy called EMDR.

Eye Movement Desensitisation and Reprocessing, as it is formally known, was developed by a California-based clinical psychologist Dr Francine Shapiro in the 1980s. One day, Dr Shapiro was taking a walk to clear her head. Distressed over some personal issue, and feeling emotional, she noticed that as she walked and moved her eyes back and forth from left to right scanning her environment, she started to feel significantly better. Was there something in the movement of her eyes back and forth that caused her emotions to be 'processed' and released, enabling her to return quickly to a state of emotional balance and calm? She was intrigued enough that she started experimenting with close friends and colleagues, eventually developing what became known as EMDR Therapy, with a specific protocol to assist clients in reducing the emotional intensity of traumatic memories. The protocol involved movement of the eyes back and forth horizontally to 'bilaterally' (both sides) stimulate the left and right hemispheres of the brain, alternately. As I would later learn, bilateral stimulation of the brain through eye movement or other means such as tapping alternate sides of the body, is a very powerful therapeutic tool indeed.

When I did my training in clinical psychology in the early 2000s, EMDR was somewhat well known, but not yet widely used. Nor was it routinely taught in postgraduate clinical psychology training programs. It was considered weird enough to be snickered at in university hallways and didn't yet have the significant scientific evidence base that it has today. Well, for all the snickering and sideways glances, Francine Shapiro's weird eye movement therapy is now the recognised gold standard for treating posttraumatic stress disorder and is completely mainstream.

In minutes and hours, EMDR does for highly emotional memories what cognitive therapy alone would take weeks and months. It can reduce the intensity of emotional distress and eliminate the most distressing elements of these memories: the 'reexperiencing' symptoms, in which the client feels like the traumatic event is happening again; and the tendency for these memories to intrude on the client's consciousness when they aren't being deliberately recalled.

It is these aspects of posttraumatic stress that make it so hard for sufferers to function. Think the Vietnam Veteran who hears a car backfire or fireworks exploding and immediately reacts as if he's back in the jungle decades ago. Severe posttraumatic stress can be debilitating.

In 1995 Dr Allan Botkin was treating PTSD in a Vietnam Veteran population – they were inpatients in a Veteran's Affairs hospital in Chicago – when he discovered IADC. Being in charge of the trauma program gave Dr Botkin the opportunity to try variations in the standard EMDR protocol, of which he was an early adoptee. He admitted 95% of his variations didn't work. But there were two crucial changes he made that did. In a presentation to the International Association of Near Death Studies (IANDS) in 2002 he described how the discovery was made[1]:

"One [change] is I have patients close their eyes after each set of eye movement. The reason I started doing that is, some of my patients I was working with, after giving them a set of eye movements, they just spontaneously closed their eyes... Those that did that got a much better response, so I started instructing all my patients to close their eyes after each set of eye movement, and they all started getting a much better response."

The other change, he said, was to focus on the sadness rather than fear, anger or guilt. He hypothesised that sadness was the core of their distress. He referred to this as 'core-focused EMDR':

"If the patient is able to access sadness even to that tiniest degree... I go right after it. I'm much more direct in my eye

movement approach than the way it's taught... I don't allow them to talk about their anger and their guilt or whatever. I explain to them ahead of time that what we do is not talk therapy, nor is it standard EMDR therapy."

Botkin's core-focused EMDR was effective not only for reducing sadness, but also the anger, guilt, and fear that his patients experienced as a result of their trauma. Because sadness was at the core, the accompanying emotions would dissolve if the sadness dissolved. Initially, eye-movement helps access the emotion, so often clients' distress would initially increase. But it would then quickly decrease. In fact, not only would clients very quickly experience a reduction in their sadness, but they would start to report good feelings emerging. They would start feeling calm and peaceful.

It was during one of Dr Botkin's usual core-focused EMDR sessions with a Vietnam veteran, that something very strange occurred. He was working with 'Sam', a client whose posttraumatic stress was so severe he was hospitalised. At the heart of his distress was an incident in which a local orphan girl, whom Sam had befriended, was shot and killed in a firefight when the Viet-Cong attacked his US Army base. As Dr Botkin describes, it was Sam's "psychological undoing".

At the beginning of the session, Sam's distress was extremely intense as he confronted the incident – and overwhelming sadness – that had rendered his life dysfunctional. As the sadness reduced, Sam reported feeling peaceful and calm – all the things Dr Botkin had come to expect. But an additional set of eye movements to help Sam relax further and enjoy his newfound feelings of peace led to Sam becoming emotional again with his eyes closed, but with an expression of surprise and awe. When Sam opened his eyes, he cautiously revealed that he had seen the girl who had died, she had spoken to him, and he felt restored by a sense of immense love combined with a feeling of being reconnected to her from the other side. Sam had experienced an after-death communication, or ADC.

ADCs are very common and spontaneously occurring in the normal population. I say *normal*, because even today they are discussed by medical and mental health professionals in pathological terms. Not because they are associated with psychopathology (mental illness) – they aren't. In fact, they overwhelmingly tend to be positive and comforting experiences, and the people experiencing them tend to be mentally healthy. Rather, the *scientism* (which you'll hear more about later) and materialist worldview of modern psychiatry and psychology struggles to accommodate experiences that transcend our traditional ways of thinking about the human condition.

At first, Dr Botkin – or, as he is affectionately known, Dr Al – had no way of knowing that this was a healing phenomenon. Nor that it would be repeatable, teachable, and lead to one of the most effective and rapidly-acting psychological therapies ever discovered. Due to its relative obscurity, a lack of research, and perhaps the unusual nature of ADCs occurring in therapy, it is still today, thirty years later, an emerging treatment option for grieving clients and is not yet known or accepted by the vast mainstream. I believe it has the potential, however, to set a new global standard for treating grief, with treatment effects and efficiency that leave traditional grief counselling approaches in its dust. But in 1995 in his therapy room with Sam, Dr Al was initially worried. Was Sam hallucinating? Was he experiencing a deep psychological disturbance? Sam slept better that night than he had in years. He thanked Dr Al profusely and recovered quickly from his grief and traumatic loss. He was soon discharged from hospital to resume a fully functional life.

Then it happened again, with another client. Then another. On checking his notes, he realised what he was doing differently in these cases. When they reported the good feelings come in, he had given them *another* set of eye movement. It was in this peaceful 'receptive' mode that ADCs would naturally occur.

Dr Al was able to reliably produce this extraordinary healing phenomenon. Clients would report experiencing the presence of the deceased person in some way, accompanied by feelings of intense love and peace. They would resume their lives without the burden of daily sadness that had robbed them of their quality of life and impaired their functioning and relationships in the present. Induced After-Death Communication Therapy was born.

In 1995, I was sixteen years old with wild ambitions to become a professional race car driver (and just maybe, if that didn't work out, I'd become a psychologist). It would be another twenty years before I came across IADC therapy, and a series of unexpected events would shake the very foundations of my life, bringing me to the precipice of my own psychological unravelling. Unlike the courageous participants in my study – whose incredible stories you're about to read – I was saved from experiencing devastating grief. But that near miss would change everything, leaving me questioning not just how to heal grief, but the very nature of life, death, and what lies beyond.

10

Chapter 3

Nanna

Years before I sat helpless on the other side of grieving clients, before my teenage racing dreams or thoughts of becoming a psychologist, I had my own early encounter with questions of loss and mortality. It happened in the most mundane of places: our laundry. Nanna was there that day, as she often was, tending to our family's washing – one of the many ways she took care of us.

I was eight years old. Most eight year-olds have a best friend. The person you wanted to play with, whose house you wanted to sleep over at, and the first person you thought of when you had free time or an exciting story to tell. For me, it was Nanna.

My dad's mum, Phylis Nehmy, grew up on a farm near Port Lincoln on South Australia's Eyre Peninsula, which she couldn't wait to escape. At seventeen she did. Nanna moved to Adelaide to become a nurse and never looked back.

Perhaps my proclivity towards psychology came from her. She was a mental health nurse at the old Glenside Hospital (a psychiatric facility) and lived in the nurse's quarters there under the watchful gaze of a domineering matron, until she met my grandfather, George Nehmy. Poppy, as we called him, was a Lebanese immigrant who went on to become a real estate agent and an aloof but ever-present background figure in my early childhood.

My earliest memories of Nanna are from when I must have been about five. Nanna and Poppy lived two streets away. Our house was a big bungalow right near Cooper's Brewery in Leabrook. The sweet, nutty, toasted scent of malt would fill the air as each batch of beer was brewed. In the afternoon of countless occasions that I would go to stay with Nanna, I recall Mum walking with me and my packed bag, up to the main road that separated our block from Nanna's. Nanna would always be there waving and smiling on the other side of the road waiting for me. Off I would trot with Nanna to Nanna and Poppy's wonderful old house to be fussed over.

To grow up having Nanna as my confidant, protector, and best friend is an experience that shaped my life beyond measure. If I could give a gift to all the children in the world it would be to have someone like her. We shared some lovely rituals when I would stay with her. She would read me stories and pat my back endlessly as I drifted off to sleep. Like a warm metronome, I couldn't have felt more loved or safe and secure. For years she would get up at my request in the middle of the night (usually when I wet the bed) to make me hot chocolates on the stove. We would eat Monte Carlo biscuits in the kitchen as the milked boiled. These became known between us as 'night biscuits'.

Nanna had developed some amazing culinary skills, which she learnt from Poppy's mother when they went to Lebanon soon after getting married. Nanna's cooking was nothing short of legendary. The flavours of my upbringing included kibbi, hommous, spinach rolls, stuffed marrows, and spiced lamb and pine nut 'cigars' baked in flaky pastry. But her tabouli was the ultimate. "Made with soft parsley" she told me one day, "not the coarse parsley most people use". In addition to the exotic flavours of her middle eastern repertoire, she also plied me with an endless supply of strawberries with icing sugar and chocolate ice cream.

Nanna was also an unwitting confederate in my truancy. I recall the day Nanna, always the devoted champion of my cause that she was, stood by watching as the boy who that morning had convinced his sceptical mother that he was too sick to go to school, rode the motorised bumper boats at Magic Mountain with glee. On another occasion, as my peers were diligently learning maths and spelling, and no doubt after my second or third bowl of strawberries with icing sugar and chocolate ice cream, I easily managed to convince Nanna that it would be a good idea for us to visit the Brickworks Market where I spent the afternoon racing indoor go-karts.

In my teens I had developed a passion for motorsport and harboured serious ambitions to become a racing driver… a fact that always seemed to draw confusion when looking at my pedigree (neither Mum nor Dad gave two hoots about car racing). But when you consider a few things about Nanna, it might not seem so strange. For all the years of dropping my brothers and I off and picking us up from school in her Commodore, it became well known that Nanna knew only two speeds: stop and flat-out. Friends walking by our street when were about to leave for school would innocently agree to a lift, only to emerge ashen-faced at the destination. And with the number of Sunday nights that she spent up late with me watching Formula One on telly, I reckon Nanna knew more about F1 than any other grandma.

My triplet brothers Alex and Chris also delighted in Nanna's care. She'd pick us up after school most days, and if we were at her house, we'd raid the jar of crown mints she kept in the living room and fight relentlessly with each other until mum arrived after work to collect us. For all the times the three of us boys stayed with Nanna and were ratbags, she always told Mum and Dad the same thing: "They were wonderful".

But Nanna and I had a special connection. If ever I was having a bad day, I would phone her up, and she would come straight away and get me. My parents ceased to be surprised when I would appear with a packed bag, right at the moment Nanna appeared at the front door. And Friday nights when my brothers were off doing other things, I would always ask to go and stay with Nanna.

Nanna called by our house almost daily, and would collect all our washing, to be returned the next day. On one occasion, amongst the load of dirty washing she took Alex's favourite ripped jeans, as was the fashion at the time. Nanna being Nanna, and much to Alex's horror, she sewed them up and returned them neatly folded and pressed.

She was a continuous and loving presence in my life. She always gave me the benefit of the doubt. Even when I seriously fucked up, she never admonished me or judged me, instead just showering me with love and affection. It's no wonder I grew up with somewhat unrealistic expectations for what it means to be loved! For a time, Nanna lived with us. She had separated from Poppy and hadn't yet found her own place. It was a happy arrangement for all of us, and I loved having her there.

One day, as Nanna was pottering in the laundry, I'd been pondering the issue of death. I was eight years old, and it had dawned on me that everyone dies, and therefore I would die, and I just couldn't imagine what that would look like or feel like. What would happen to me? Would I cease to exist? What about my parents and brothers and school friends, everyone I loved and cared for? Would it all just be gone? Worried and confused, I sprung the question on Nanna as she loaded washing into the machine.

"Nanna, what happens when we die?", I asked nervously. She sighed deeply, and looked at me sympathetically, before returning her focus to the tangle of clothes she was wrestling with.

"Oh Tommy dear, it's just like going to sleep. You go to sleep, but you don't wake up. But you don't need to worry about that, it won't be for a very, very long time."

I tried to imagine what it would be like to go to sleep but not wake up. Somehow, I couldn't quite grasp it. Did she mean I would be feeling... *nothing*? I tried to imagine experiencing nothing and felt a knot of fear rising in my stomach. I was going to be stuck in a perpetual state of *nothing*, forever! And, what's worse, I couldn't even wake up from it! How could we all be here, so alive, with so many urgent and competing thoughts and priorities. And then, one day, it's just finished. Would this really happen to *me*? I'd be here and then I'd cease to exist at all? Why?

Nanna's explanation didn't satisfy me, it just made me more anxious. I tried to push it out of my mind, reminding myself of my mum's earnest reassurance that my death would be a long, long, time away, when I was very, *very* old, and I didn't even need to worry about it now. But the fear of death lingered with me.

From the age of twelve, I started asking my parents to take me to new-age bookshops. The internet didn't exist yet, and I needed to find out more about the concept of death and a possible afterlife. I still felt anxious when I thought about death, yet I'd all but abandoned the going to sleep forever explanation – it just didn't feel right. I usually contemplated the thought at the worst possible time, right as I was meant to go to sleep! Hence, I was often awake later than I should have been.

I noticed that if I laid really still, my body would start to feel heavy and numb, and I'd feel 'waves' of tingling from head to toe, or sometimes a pulsing sensation in time with my heartbeat. I didn't know what it was, but it felt like... *energy*. If I relaxed as my body was doing this and looked slightly upwards under closed eyelids toward the top of my head, I would begin to spin. Part disorienting and part pleasant, it felt as if I might float away. Although my physical body was still, I felt like a rolling ball of energy moving through the cosmos. Another time, it felt as if pairs of disembodied hands were gently resting on my arms and legs, sending pleasant, calming tingles right through me.

I didn't know how to explain any of this, so I read books on astral travel, spirit guides and reincarnation. It would be years before I was trained as a clinical psychologist and began conducting scientific research of my own. But for now, the scientific validity of these concepts was of no concern to me. I was just looking for answers.

Why am I here?

Does a spiritual world really exist?

What's going to happen to me when I die?

My first experience of someone dying came one afternoon when the home phone in the kitchen rang. When I answered, a male voice I didn't recognise asked in a serious tone if he could speak to my mother.

Poppy had died.

I can't say it really affected me much because he and Nanna had long been separated and he'd moved back to Lebanon years before. There was no funeral, no ceremony. I don't even remember anyone even talking about it much at all. Poppy and my dad had long been estranged; they had never really gotten along. So, it was more of a gradual fading out of our lives than a sudden death. I loved him, and I knew he loved me and my brothers, but I never felt like I really *knew* him.

If there was one death that I knew would really affect me, it was going to be Nanna. Even as a young boy I became aware that she was ageing and would one day die. Whenever I thought about it, I would get a horrible sick feeling in my stomach. I would quickly push the thoughts back down. They were too much to bear.

Not only had Nanna been my best friend growing up, but as I got older and she got old, I relished the opportunity to take care of her in little ways. Once I'd earned my drivers' license, I'd show up in the late afternoon with crumbed fish and chips for her dinner from her favourite take away shop. I could help her work her video recorder, or call the phone company on her behalf. More than anything though, she just loved my random visits. We loved each other very much, but there was something special about our connection that went beyond love and affection.

On one of my usual visits to her little house in the foothills east of Adelaide, Nanna was not her normal self. She seemed irritable. Not exactly *at me*, but irritable nonetheless. Nanna loved me coming to visit, so it was strange that she was grumpy. She was not an overly social lady and didn't often have visitors. My usual visits would break up the monotony of her quiet days. She'd make a cup of tea and we'd sit and talk. I'm not trying to toot my own horn, but she *loved* seeing me. So her being irritable when she answered the door and I stepped into the loungeroom was *weird*.

Not only was Nanna acting strange, she also said something that really spooked me: she'd dreamt of Poppy the night before. By this stage, Nanna and Poppy had been separated for over twenty years, and he'd been dead for ten. We didn't avoid talking about him, he just didn't often come up in conversation. A strange feeling overwhelmed me that something wasn't right with Nanna.

I didn't linger that day. My head was swirling trying to figure out what was going on with her. She didn't report any pain and physically she seemed fine. But my feeling of unease grew as I mindlessly steered my silver Ford Laser hatchback the five-minute drive home.

Something was wrong!

I pulled into the driveway as Mum was getting home, noticing the ashen look on my face. "I think Nanna's going to die," I blurted, unable to stop my bottom lip from trembling.

When Mum gave me that truly kind, concerned look that loving mothers give, I couldn't hold it back anymore. I stood next to my car with slumped shoulders and tears streaming down my cheeks. I couldn't explain to Mum exactly *what* was wrong with her. It was just a *feeling*.

She reassured me that Nanna was fine. And feeling comforted, I started to doubt myself. Maybe Nanna was just having an off day. She was old, after all. We had suspected a bit of dementia was setting in. I pushed my concerns aside, convinced she'd be back to normal when I visited her again the next week.

But two days later, Dad rang to tell me Nanna was in hospital. She had collapsed at home, and they'd found blood on her carpeted loungeroom floor. I was right, something had been wrong! Nanna had been unwell, but thankfully my prediction didn't come true – she didn't die.

Only a few months later I was driving home (too fast as usual), having left uni where I was doing my undergrad studies in psychology, when the *feeling* returned. I had an overwhelming urge to drive to Nanna.

I'd called in to her place just the day before, still impressed by the way she'd cheated death despite my certainty that it was near. But now I had a sudden sense of pressure in my stomach and forehead – a combination of feeling focused, determined, and having an itch you have to scratch right now – all at the same time. I sped up, weaving through the traffic. My hatchback's sports exhaust sounding even louder than usual as I raced through the backstreets, looking for shortcuts. I was wrong last time, I told myself. Hopefully I'd be wrong again. When I got to the front door, Nanna was her usual old self, smiling as she kissed me on the cheek. What a relief!

I sunk into her old brown leather couch in the loungeroom, chiding myself on being overly anxious, when I smelt gas. Hurrying to the kitchen, the smell was so strong I could almost taste it. It wasn't hard to find the culprit: a gas burner on the stove was going full bore, without a flame. I quickly flipped the knob off and checked the rest of the burners were off too. Nanna must have gone to cook something and gotten distracted, never lighting it. I opened all the windows and doors and quickly ushered Nanna outside onto her paved courtyard.

It was another close call. Dad started looking into nursing homes when it became clear that Nanna needed more support and probably wasn't safe living on her own.

And I wondered what the hell was going on with my newfound intuition.

After Nanna moved into the nursing home, I continued to visit her regularly. She wasn't keen on giving up her independence but also knew she was declining. Getting old can be a cruel bastard of a thing, but it is the absolute and unavoidable course of nature.

Well, the nature of getting old was on full display at the nursing home. And you could smell it too. What was it with the smell? And why was it so hot in there? Couldn't they open a window?

The nursing staff were amazing. I thanked and admired them. But I breathed a deep sigh of relief whenever I hit the cool fresh air as I was leaving. Partly it was about the smell and the heat, but mostly it was a newfound gratitude for the youth I took for granted. Somewhere beneath the surface was the lingering fear of death, the uncertainty of what comes next, and all the other questions I was still searching for answers to. It only lasted a moment, though. The programming of my eight-year-old brain reassured me that my death was surely a long, long way away, when I would be very, very old.

After almost two years in the nursing home, Nanna's gradual decline became more obvious: forgetting people's names, having repetitive conversations, finding it harder to move, eat, and get out of bed. Quietly proud that I was one of the few people Nanna would immediately recognise, I was dreading the day I would walk into her room, and she'd ask, "Who are you?"

Having been getting progressively weaker as she aged – and now 84 years old – Nanna developed pneumonia. She wasn't really eating or drinking and was sleeping a lot. It looked like she was in some kind of coma. I felt uneasy in the room with her like that. Almost like I was trespassing, even though in a way it was like she wasn't really there.

Over the coming days Dad's fatherly instincts were protective: he gently tried to dissuade me from coming in to the nursing home, knowing how distressing it would be for me. She was being well looked after, and she was really just sleeping anyway, he assured me. I hoped she'd bounce back from this illness as she had done many times before, but we both knew the end could be near.

A few days later I was grappling with the decision of whether to go in to the nursing home. I was in the midst of my new job as a clinical psychologist and the usual busy-ness of life. I resolved I'd visit her very soon – sometime in the next day or two – I just wasn't sure when. She was still sleeping, Dad assured me. So I pushed thoughts of Nanna to the back of my mind in order to get through the demands of the day.

Later that afternoon, I was at home when very suddenly I had the overwhelming *feeling* that I needed to go to Nanna. It wasn't that I started thinking about her and became panicked. It was as if the feeling came to me. My heart started racing. It was the same feeling I'd had when Nanna had left the gas on the stove... a sense of undeniable urgency and the anticipation of something otherworldly occurring. I just knew. I had to go to Nanna.

I scrambled to grab my wallet and keys. Where were my keys? I was racing around the house as the adrenaline that always comes with the feeling coursed through my body.

Where are my fucking keys?!

I never lose my keys. I'm just not that person. They're always by the fruit bowl in the kitchen. I dashed around and retraced my steps again. Five damn minutes. They were upstairs on the edge of the desk by the landing. I raced back down and jumped the final few stairs, dashing out to my car.

My heart was still pounding as I walked briskly into the nursing home and went straight to Nanna's room without speaking to the staff. As I burst into Nanna's room, I saw my Dad bent forward next to her bed, crying. I'd never seen my dad cry before. I looked to Nanna in her bed, with the covers pulled up to her chin. Her eyes that had sparkled at me warmly with unconditional love and acceptance over so many years were half open, but they looked different.

Nanna had died one minute before.

Chapter 4

Eleanor

Eleanor arrived for her appointment early, with an air of country charm about her. But despite her polite and friendly chit-chat, as she sat down in the red armchair in my small rented consulting room, it was clear she was carrying a heavy burden.

Her husband of 49 years, Mark, had died only eight months prior from Idiopathic Pulmonary Fibrosis. "His lungs were like glass," she had told me tearfully on our screening call. "The specialist gave him five years, but we didn't get as much time as we expected." Eleanor and Mark had the kind of relationship most of us hope for: dedicated, loving, constant, unwavering. Although she had time to prepare for his death, it was still a shock to suddenly find herself on her own. Life had always been about them as a pair, and now it was just Eleanor. She was "floating between" her three kids' residences, and although she enjoyed the support of her loving family, she was depressed and struggling. Not wanting to make a fuss or burden her family with her grief, Eleanor bottled it up. Grief counselling had given her someone to talk to other than family, but it hadn't been enough for her to heal in any significant way. Eleanor was from a generation that wouldn't want to make a fuss, yet sometimes her grief was so intense, she confided in me, "Sometimes I just want to scream."

Once Eleanor was settled, I explained what we'd be doing during our first ninety-minute session, and we practiced the tapping technique we would use during the IADC therapy. I noticed that as she began talking about Mark, Eleanor's expression became sombre, her voice lowered as her hands fidgeted with the hem of her shirt. As she described her loss, I had an image of her life being split in two parts. The part with Mark's continuous loving presence ("He was always there, he was always supportive, we did everything together"), and the part that now felt foreign, confusing, and stressful.

I asked Eleanor if she could identify the strongest 'piece' of sadness. Pieces of sadness are the emotional hot buttons that define a client's current grief. They can be specific (the moment I got the phone call to say my loved one had died), or general (I miss him). They can include distressing images (like the moment a casket is lowered into the ground), sounds, or even future concerns. For Eleanor, was it facing the prospect of her later years on her own? Was it the loss of Mark's companionship and affection after so many years? There were many layers to Eleanor's grief, but for therapy to be most effective we needed to find where it was most intense for her *right now*.

Worst first is the principle underpinning IADC therapy, which is why it isn't for the faint hearted. We follow whichever is the most intense piece of sadness in that moment, and – as Dr Botkin would say – "go after it". As an IADC therapist it is my job to be relentless until we break through to the other side, where peace and acceptance reside. I knew Eleanor was going to be exhausted at the end of this first ninety-minute appointment, and I wanted it to be worth it.

"The strongest part," she said, "is just the loneliness. He's left me."

I instructed her to start tapping, just as we had practiced earlier. Eleanor was using the butterfly hug method of bilateral stimulation, alternately tapping each shoulder with arms crossed over her chest. It didn't take long to fully access her sadness. One of the things that bilateral stimulation does very well, is unlock emotions that are stored in the limbic system of the brain. Like a dam wall breaking, the sadness that she was trying so hard to manage in her daily life suddenly burst forth with such intensity that her whole body shook. Guttural sobs interspersed with stuttered breaths accompanied the seemingly endless stream of tears flowing from her closed eyes.

I needed her to keep tapping, even if it felt overwhelming. "Keep going, Eleanor, keep going," I quietly encouraged her, but loud enough that she could hear me through her sobs. It was important that no matter how intense, we continue the processing through the peaks of her distress. Traditional EMDR takes clients to a 'safe place' when their emotions feel overwhelming, but the IADC therapy protocol sees this as an abortive process, effectively taking the client out of precisely where they need to be: feeling the full intensity of their emotions.

As is common in IADC therapy, Eleanor's sadness initially increased as she accessed the stored emotion, and for three consecutive sets of tapping she processed wave after wave of sadness, until eventually, she reported returning to "normal crying" rather than the gut-wrenching surges of the early sets. "The first time I felt like it was just a big ball of sadness," she said. "Now the sadness doesn't feel as intense, and it feels like there's something comforting about the tears."

I was happy with the progress made in the first day's session. I reminded Eleanor that some processing would continue even after we had stopped the formal sets of bilateral stimulation for the day. There seems to be momentum after an IADC session that allows further gains to naturally occur. I also told her that she was likely to experience further gains after sleeping that night, when she would go through the rapid eye movement (REM) phases of sleep.

When Eleanor returned the next day for her second session, she was surprised at the profound impact of the first session. For a few hours the afternoon before, she had felt much better, like she hadn't in months. "I've been in a dream, almost. And yesterday, for those few hours, I felt like I was awake and sharp. And then once I started to get really tired the fogginess came back, and the disorientation, I couldn't find where I was. I've been living with that fogginess for the last… I don't know how long," she said with a hopeful tone in her voice.

It wasn't uncommon for grief clients to describe themselves as being lost in a fog, to have trouble concentrating, or to simply feel fatigued or disoriented in all manner of situations. The heavy emotions encoded in their brains, and being reactivated day after day, is not only draining of physical and emotional energy, it consumes mental energy too. Psychologists call this mental effort a 'cognitive load': it's like part of a computer's processing power being consumed by software running in the background. The continual activation of parts of the brain associated with grief consumes mental resources and applies a handbrake to all the other thinking that needs to be done.

Now Eleanor was already experiencing relief from the fogginess. I tried to hide it, but I felt the weight of expectation on my shoulders. Eleanor had shown such extraordinary courage to step into the full burn of that intense distress, putting her trust in me, a perfect stranger. I couldn't let her down.

We started our session, the second of two. Eleanor was able to access more sadness, but it wasn't as intense as the day before. After a few sets of bilateral stimulation, she reported feeling less sad. After five sets, she felt calm. I had come to expect that eventually she would report feeling very calm, relaxed, or peaceful. After seven sets, she felt acceptance. These are the hallmark indicators that a client is going into a receptive mode in which an ADC could occur.

After nine sets of tapping, she opened her eyes and looked at me apprehensively as she reached for more tissues on the table next to her. "This is going to sound really strange. There's just a purple light sitting there. It makes me feel good."

"Eleanor, if you're seeing a purple light and feeling good it means you're getting into a nice receptive mode now," I reassured her. Seeing vivid colours beneath closed eyelids usually indicates an ADC is unfolding. I didn't want to inadvertently move her into her left brain (thinking rather than feeling) by asking questions. I just wanted her to relax into it and let it happen naturally. "We've processed the sadness, and now we'll just go into the good feeling. Think about Mark in a general way, and just notice whatever happens. Just be open to anything. We don't have to force anything. Just let it unfold."

After another set of tapping, Eleanor whispered, "A white orb keeps coming in and around. There's still the purple light, but this white orb keeps coming down. The purple light is so perfect, and the white orb keeps coming down into it."

I never want to impose my interpretation on my client regarding what they're experiencing, so I asked Eleanor what it meant to her.

"Something's there. And if it's Mark, stop playing around with me!" she chuckled softly. Eleanor suddenly looked happier, lighter, as she contemplated the positive emotions she was feeling, and what it all meant. It struck me that her outward expression of emotion – what psychologists call the client's 'affect' – had changed so drastically in just twenty-four hours. We were still focused on the death of her beloved husband, but now she was able to smile while talking about him.

Before we started the next set, I instructed Eleanor to keep her eyes closed for as long as she was noticing anything happening, even after she had stopped tapping. "Don't force anything, just let it come to you," I reminded her. After the tapping stopped, Eleanor kept her eyes closed. Then, after about 30 seconds, still with eyes closed, she started crying again. Her breathing intensified with emotion, as her head bobbed gently from side to side as she attended to her private experience. I had noticed this 'floating head' phenomenon when my clients were deeply relaxed and able to focus on their internal sensations.

Eleanor sounded slightly breathless, excited at what she was experiencing. "The white orb came in and all around me. Then slowly but surely floating off again."

"Was there a feeling that came with the orb?" I gently probed.

"Calm…. Love… Maybe a little bit of strength," she said. We did another set to see if the experience continued, and eventually she opened her eyes. "I think he's gone," Eleanor said softly as she reached for more tissues. "I feel peaceful," she added.

We sat and chatted for a while. It was remarkable to observe the transformation in how she presented clinically (her mood, level of distress) from the beginning of our first session the day before, until now. The sheer speed of therapeutic progress was remarkable. She described a feeling of love washing over her – a description I had heard before from other IADC clients. But I wasn't just familiar with it from client stories. I knew exactly what that felt like. I had experienced my own spontaneous ADCs which brought waves of comfort and love that transcended mere reassurance. They came from a *presence*! I knew Eleanor was feeling her husband right there with her.

It didn't matter that I was exhausted, that I was sitting in this stuffy little office on a Sunday after working a fifty-hour week. It didn't matter that these sessions were just one part of a whole lot more work I'd have to do for this major university research project to evaluate IADC therapy. It didn't matter that I wasn't getting paid. None of that mattered one bit. If I could give Eleanor the experience of feeling close to Mark again… how could I *not*?

"It means everything to me because I know that he's there," Eleanor's eyes were earnest now with relief and gratitude. "I knew that before, but I haven't been feeling him close to me, and now I *know* he's there."

As I reflected on Eleanor's remarkable improvement, it occurred to me that the changes I observed in her in just two ninety-minute sessions on consecutive days, were greater than the improvement I'd seen in many clients undergoing ten to twenty sessions of cognitive behaviour therapy for anxiety and depression. It wasn't just deeply satisfying; in a strange way it was almost addictive. I now had something that worked well – and fast. No longer was I dreading grief-stricken clients, I was seeking them out.

Chapter 5

After-Death Communication

I t hurt when Nanna died, but I didn't cry that much. As sad as I was, she was at the end of her natural life. She was 84 years old and had spent over a decade reminding me weekly: "Don't get old, Tommy!". I resolved not to torture myself over arriving at the nursing home one minute late and not being at her bedside when she died. In hindsight, I believe that moment was meant for Dad.

But her death did make me ponder the topic of death more deeply. At 27 years old, I'd (thankfully) been to hardly any funerals, which made the experience of dealing with Nanna's funeral all the more confronting: choosing coffins, burying or cremating, writing eulogies. It was so far removed from my ordinary life of twentysomething friends, parties, girls, work, and everything else that consumed my time and energy.

Solemn music played in the funeral home chapel as we entered. Seeing the coffin at the end of the aisle with light streaming in through the big stained-glass windows felt sad, but also strange. I couldn't help but wonder, was she really in there? The question loomed large in my mind: if the essence of Nanna wasn't in her body, which was dead: where *was* she? I'd read and experienced too much to believe that death was the end. I'd resolved that Nanna's sleep hypothesis, which had disturbed me all those years ago, couldn't possibly be true. It just didn't feel right at all. But still, where was she? If we live on in an afterlife, then surely Nanna would come and visit me, to let me know she's okay. If anyone would, it'd be her.

But the following year came and went, and there was nothing. No visions, no dreams. No strange coincidences or messages or feathers appearing on my pillow. Just a stillness and a longing whenever I thought of her.

My hope to hear from Nanna after her death was not unfounded. Research tells us that getting a visit from a deceased loved one is common. In fact, after-death communications are *very* common. If you walked down a busy street tapping people on the shoulder and asking them if they had ever perceived the presence of a deceased person, around one in three would say 'yes'[2]. And despite these experiences being pathologised in medical textbooks as 'grief hallucinations', they are overwhelmingly positive, comforting experiences[3].

The term after-death communication was coined by Bill and Judy Guggenheim when they painstakingly researched over 3,300 cases and interviewed more than 200 subjects. In their 1995 bestselling book *Hello from Heaven*[4], they listed 12 types of ADCs:

> **Sensing a Presence:** Feeling the presence of the deceased nearby, often described as a strong, unmistakable sense that they are with you.

> **Hearing a Voice:** Hearing the audible voice of the deceased, either externally (as if spoken aloud) or internally (as a thought or telepathic communication).

> **Feeling a Touch:** Experiencing a physical touch from the deceased, such as a hand on the shoulder or a gentle caress.

Smelling a Fragrance: Detecting a distinct fragrance associated with the deceased, like their favourite perfume, flowers, or even tobacco smoke.

Visual Experiences: Seeing a full or partial appearance of the deceased, either in a dream-like state, a vision, or as a solid apparition.

Twilight Experiences: Having an ADC while falling asleep, waking up, or in a relaxed state, where the deceased may appear in a vision or communicate.

Dreams / Sleep ADCs: Receiving messages or visits from the deceased in vivid, memorable dreams that stand out from ordinary dreams.

Out-of-Body Experiences: Encountering the deceased during an out-of-body experience (OBE), where the experiencer leaves their physical body and meets the deceased.

Telephone Calls or Text Messages: Receiving a phone call or text message from the deceased, the caller's voice may be recognised, and messages are conveyed.

Physical Phenomena: Witnessing physical events that are attributed to the deceased, such as moving objects, lights flickering, or other unexplained occurrences.

Symbolic ADCs: Receiving signs or symbols that are meaningful and clearly connected to the deceased, such as seeing their favourite bird, numbers, or other personal symbols repeatedly.

Other Unusual Experiences: Various other unique experiences that don't fit the other categories.

Once Dr Botkin's clients started spontaneously reporting the presence of the deceased people they were grieving, it was the Guggenheims' work that prompted him to change the name of his Core Focused EMDR into Induced After Death Communication Therapy. As I was to discover many years later, the bilateral stimulation in EMDR, combined with the focus on sadness (and a few other crucial factors), would put individuals into a 'receptive state' in which ADCs were likely to occur. I would also discover that the natural bilateral stimulation of REM sleep can activate this receptive state too.

Nearly two years had passed since Nanna's death when one morning, lying in bed with my eyes closed, I saw her! She looked younger – about sixty years old – with her wavy auburn curls, sparkling blue eyes and bright red lipstick. She was smiling. I felt a wave of love wash over me. There was no sense of being anywhere in particular; it was just Nanna and me. With the rush of excitement that comes from something so special and unusual happening, I mentally said to her, "Nanna! You look really good!" She just smiled. And as suddenly as she was there, she was gone.

I laid there for a few moments with my eyes still closed, alone in my bed as the first rays of sunlight crept through the blinds, trying to grasp that moment, trying to hold on to her presence. It was only then that I realised my face and pillow were drenched with tears.

Finally, it had happened!

I wasn't imagining Nanna. I definitely wasn't dreaming… I had been asleep, but there was no sense of coming out of a dream or being in a dream state. (It felt entirely different from a dream). I was fully lucid and aware in that moment. It was really her!

I learned later that it is very common for the deceased to appear younger in ADCs than when they died. Mum told me that sixty was the age Nanna was happiest, helping look after me and my brothers, focusing on family, enjoying being someone we depended on in little ways all the time.

It wasn't the last time I would get a visit from Nanna.

Eighteen months later, I was getting ready for bed at about 10pm, folding some clothes into my suitcase to be ready for my early flight to Sydney the next morning. I was attending the Sydney Cup – one of Australia's most prestigious horse races – as a co-owner of one of the runners, eight-year-old gelding Ista Kareem.

Ista Kareem, or 'Hermie' as we called him, had been purchased by my dad as a two-year-old in New Zealand. Dad's passion for many years was studying bloodlines and breeding racehorses. Hermie had won the Launceston Cup only fourteen months before, which helped him gain entry into the Group 1, two-mile Sydney Cup. At the time, it was the jewel of the Sydney racing calendar, surpassed only in prestige by the world-famous Melbourne Cup (known as 'the race that stops a nation').

I was packing the last few things I needed in anticipation of the 5.30am arrival of my taxi to take me to the airport, when the atmosphere shifted in the room. It was such a powerful sensation that I stood still. Tingles ran up and down my spine as Nanna's presence surrounded me.

"Nanna, you're here!" I said out loud, my heart racing.

I didn't see anything, and I didn't get an audible reply. But the *feeling* of her presence was almost overwhelming. It had barely occurred to me to ask *why* she was there when another wave of tingles washed over me.

And then I knew.

"We're going to win, aren't we?" I said out loud again in my quiet bedroom, with a tone of wonder and certainty. Then the feeling faded away.

I pulled the doona up and switched out the light, having checked that my early-morning alarm was set, feeling an inner warmth from the certainty of knowing she was still with me.

As I made my way into the bustling Royal Randwick Racecourse in Sydney's eastern suburbs, I had butterflies. The Sydney Cup was a huge day on the racing calendar. Even by eleven a.m. there were betting ticket stubs littering the ground, trodden on by a thousand high heels worn by glamorously dressed women with suited men in tow.

It didn't take long to find Dad, when soon after a bugle call rang out. It was ANZAC Day, a national public holiday in Australia commemorating the brave service of the Australian and New Zealand Army Corps. The haunting sounds of *The Last Post* swirled as punters stopped and gentlemen removed their hats. An eerie stillness descended on what only moments before had been a heaving hive of activity. The butterflies got stronger.

I wondered what Dad would think if I told him about Nanna's visit. Naah, he wouldn't believe me, I thought. Dad wasn't really into metaphysical stuff, but he was happy to support my interest in it. I had a glass of champagne to calm my nerves. We spoke to our jockey Craig Williams in the mounting yard. Ride him back and let him settle was the plan. Relax and take cover until the time was right. Hermie was a true stayer. A finisher. He was made for two-mile races.

Racetracks are so big, I'd normally rely on the race caller, or the big screen (if they had one), to follow the action. I was never any good at following with binoculars. Thankfully, Royal Randwick did have a big screen, and due to the length of the race, the field would pass the finishing straight twice, meaning we'd get to see Hermie up close from our spot in the main grandstand.

By the time they jumped, the butterflies in my stomach were having a party. Just as we'd agreed, Craig Williams let Hermie relax.

He settled about two thirds of the way back in the field, one off the rail. They passed the post for the first time, eliciting cheers from the crowd. So far, so good.

He stayed in position until they passed the 800m mark when the field started to bunch up. Jockeys were looking for room and the tempo increased. Coming down the home straight, it was nearly impossible to make out Hermie from the rest of the field. He looked to be about halfway back in the pack of jostling horses and flying whips. With only a few hundred metres to go, the race caller was now only calling the horses at the front.

I was crestfallen. Does this mean Nanna wasn't right? Or, worse than that, had I imagined the whole thing? I'd placed a bloody big bet too!

I looked over to Dad who seemed to be mesmerised by the action in front of him. He understood this game much better than me. I just went along for the fun. For just a moment, it seemed like the roaring crowd had faded away as I pondered the implications of this day for Dad, for me, and what it all meant about my visits from Nanna. Perhaps after-death communications were just something wishful that people made up in their own heads.

I looked back to the raging mass of horses, trying somehow to make out Hermie in the swirling palette of chestnut horse hair, jockey colours and caps. By the time the pack reached the two hundred metre mark the crowd was screaming. I tried to make out the race caller's excited tones. I didn't hear him mention Ista Kareem.

"Mr Tipsy!.... and Lang is coming down the outside as well!... Divine Rebel and Mr Tipsy!.... Mr Tipsy!"

For a moment it looked as if Craig Williams, in our family's colours including a white and blue spotted cap, appeared on the inside. Was that Hermie? The racecaller's voice had already reached the 'get me a defibrillator' level when it hit another octave altogether, and the energy of the crowd rose with it. The noise was deafening.

"And now… Ista Kareem is charging along the inside!
Ista Kareem is flyyy-ing!
And won the Sydney Cup for Williams!"
We'd won.

Everyone was screaming, my heart was pounding, and amidst all the jumping up and down and hugging and more screaming I felt an emotional tingle all over, just like the night before when the otherworldly wave of Nanna's presence had washed over me. My phone buzzed incessantly in my pocket. The race was televised live around the country, and friends and family were calling and texting their congratulations.

It was an amazing feeling to win the Sydney Cup. I was beyond thrilled to be with my dad on the day one of his life dreams was coming true. And I now had social permission to drink my bodyweight in champagne. But, as we walked down to the weigh-in area with TV cameras, backslapping, and hugs from strangers, I realised something even more important had occurred: Nanna was right.

Her visit was real.

A year later, I was firmly ensconced in adult professional life. Well, sort of. I had moved back in with my mum temporarily, but now had a busy private practice and had started a PhD trying to develop an effective prevention program for anxiety, depression, and eating disorders (this would later become the Healthy Minds program used in schools and companies around Australia). I'd also managed to turn a dalliance with an Austrian girl into plans for a month-long trip to Europe.

It all started the night before Christmas Eve when my best mate Corey and I hit the town. I overheard two cute girls speaking in German as they smoked a cigarette. Despite the fact that it was near closing time at The Exeter Hotel and I'd already had more than enough fun for one evening, I thought it was a chance to put three years of high school German Studies to the test.

A whirlwind... something... ensued. I'm not sure it was enough to call a romance – it was too brief – but enough that when she returned to Austria, we could idealise each other, and we stayed in touch planning our reunion.

Eight days before I was due to depart, she emailed to say she'd met someone. With the click of a mouse button, all the plans I had were down the drain. Do I go... on my own? I didn't have any accommodation booked. And now I had no plans to see anyone or do anything, other than attend a Maria Mena concert in Switzerland... with her. I had to decide quickly.

All kinds of mixed thoughts and emotions were swirling in my head as I drove my Holden Astra back to Mum's after a trip to the shops. Do I book a tour? Was I too old for Contiki? In the middle of that thought, the atmosphere changed. Yes, I was doing sixty km/h in my car, but it changed nonetheless.

Nanna was back!

Just like the night before the Sydney Cup there were no words spoken, just the feeling. It was unmistakably her. Nanna was telling me it was okay to go. Everything would work out alright.

And work out it did. After Nanna's visit I resolved that I would go on that trip, I'd say yes to everything, and introduce myself to everyone. It turns out I wasn't too old for Contiki. I went to that Maria Mena concert with a random but lovely lady I met in Lucerne, Switzerland. I visited Mozart's statue in Salzburg. I jumped off sailboats into the azure blue waters off the Adriatic Sea near Croatia. And I partied in Berlin.

Nanna was right again. I had the time of my life.

A couple of years later, I was finally embracing adulthood in a serious way. I bought a house. Well, half a house.

Corey and I resolved to buy a house together, as on our own we could only afford something pretty crappy. It would be a minimum two-year arrangement. There might even be some tax benefits if we told the mortgage broker we were gay. (We didn't).

The criteria for our new abode? Two living areas, two bathrooms... and a jacuzzi. And no matter what, no girls were allowed to move in. (Neither of us consulted a lawyer, but we figured if one of us had a girlfriend move in, she might be able to claim some of the asset if the relationship broke up).

My PhD was progressing well, I was seeing clients, running corporate training workshops, and generally having fun. Life was sweet. Visits from deceased loved ones were the furthest thing from my mind.

Then one Sunday morning, Mum rang.

"Hi Darling, I just wanted to let you know that Grandpa is quite unwell. Perhaps you could see him today?" Mum asked.

My mum's parents, Nanny and Grandpa, were both warm, kind, presences in my life. When we were kids they'd often pick us up after school until Mum got home from her job as a teacher. Nanny would make us tea and toast, and Grandpa would quiz us with maths problems, or throw a tennis ball from the balcony for us to catch in the backyard.

I had never asked Nanny or Grandpa about death because although I loved them very much, I wasn't as close with them as with Nanna, and I didn't spend much one-on-one time with either of them to have those kinds of discussions. Unlike my regular sleepovers at Nanna's house, my brothers were usually around when we visited Nanny and Grandpa, and us boys would end up playing wrestle mania in the back yard or generally horsing around.

"No problem," I told Mum, and later that afternoon I drove to the War Veterans' home where Grandpa and Nanny lived.

The thing about Grandpa was, he never made a fuss. He had been a fighter pilot in World War Two, an entrepreneur, an accountant, and many other things. Now ninety-five, he had developed something called Paget's Disease, a painful condition in which bones become deformed. It affected his hips and would have been torturous at times. But he never complained.

This particular Sunday was no different. While clearly unwell, Grandpa still smiled, propped up slightly on his pillows in bed, grateful for my visit. In fact, I didn't realise quite how unwell Grandpa was. By evening, his eyes were closed and his breathing was laboured. My uncle and cousin came in to see him. Mum and Nanny were pottering around his room and chatting when I noticed Grandpa's breathing had slowed considerably.

"I think it might be a good time to come and sit with Grandpa," I said softly, trying not to let my voice crack with emotion. I wanted to be strong for Mum. She and Grandpa had always been very close.

When Grandpa had appeared to take his last breath, there was a strange moment of peace, followed by a little panic. Was there something we should do? In the moment, there was nothing much to be done except give our thanks for a very full life and a special soul. Grandpa had been a kind and protective figure in all our lives, and we loved him dearly.

Ten days after Grandpa died, I was coming out of sleep, with no sense of having been in a dream, when I saw him! It was unmistakenly him! But this time, he looked much younger than when he died; about thirty years old.

And he spoke to me.

Not as in speaking with your mouth moving, but a telepathic communication. It felt as natural as speaking with your mouth and I knew exactly what he was saying.

"In my life, I got to experience everything!"

Grandpa's presence was loving, but more than that, he was emitting a feeling of being satisfied. He was celebrating the life he'd had in his physical body as Grandpa, deeply content not with specific achievements, but with the breadth of his experience.

I pondered Grandpa's words. The fact that they were so unexpected reassured me that this had been a real communication: in a million years, if I was concocting messages in my own mind for what I expected Grandpa to say to me after his death, that wouldn't have been it. As for the meaning of Grandpas message? This would make more sense to me later as I read and studied hundreds of cases of near-death-experiences, in which people report the experience of dying, having a life review, and returning to their bodies after being resuscitated. Grandpa's visit left me with a sense of deep peace.

Nanny, my mum's mum, was 103 when she died. When she was born, they drove her home in a trap and buggy. She lived through the Great Depression, two world wars, the birth of computer technology, the internet, and even self-driving cars.

Nanny was a matriarch in a quiet way. Family always came first. She loved Grandpa, her kids (my mum and uncle), her five grandkids, and four great-grandkids. Nobody made a better lamb roast. And although she had predicted since about the age of sixty-five that it would be her "last Christmas", Nanny had an unbelievable run of good health and good fortune, until the very end.

About a week after she died, as I was coming out of sleep early in the morning – without any sense of dreaming – I was suddenly awake and aware with my eyes closed, looking at Nanny smiling. She looked about sixty years old, with bright eyes, wearing a pendant necklace. She was very happy!

Unlike the visits from Nanna and Grandpa, Nanny and I actually touched. She gave me a big hug! Her love and happiness radiated through me as I felt her arms wrap around me, pulling me close. Wherever she was now, she wasn't frail and battling the ravages of old age. She was vibrant, healthy, and very content. I felt that she wanted me to know how happy and well she was.

The deaths of my grandparents, and their subsequent visits, taught me two vital lessons. First, after-death communications are healing. Feeling the presence of our loved ones after their passing is immensely reassuring; a form of spiritual intimacy that reflects our continued bonds of love and influence. While these visits can't completely erase grief, as they don't replace the physical absence of a loved one, they do heal our deepest fear: that our loved ones are gone forever, lost to us, and cease to exist. Which brings us to the second lesson: there is no death. At least not in the way we conceive it. There is a life beyond the physical, and it is more awe-inspiring than we can imagine.

Chapter 6

Samantha

Samantha volunteered to participate in my research because grief had become the "underlying current" of her life since her husband, John, died of a rare form of cancer four and a half years earlier. She maintained a busy life as an accomplished management consultant and now single mother to her seventeen-year-old daughter Emma, but she wanted help with her grief because it felt like she was "never going to get rid of it".

Two things intrigued me about Samantha's story.

She had deeply loved John but had mixed feelings about their marriage because, while he was "good ninety-five percent of the time", he had, at times, been controlling and abusive. She told me she'd recently come to the conclusion that had their marriage not been interrupted by his illness and death, she would have left him.

And… she'd already felt his presence multiple times since he died.

When they first met at a conference, Samantha and John had talked non-stop. Samantha was drawn in by his charisma and intelligence, and even from the very first meeting she had a feeling that they'd be together forever. "I felt like I belonged somewhere, with him. I loved him deeply. But he had a terrible temper."

Samantha was ready to start a new chapter. She was accomplished, attractive, and with the prospect of her soon-to-be-adult daughter leaving home to live overseas, her world should have been opening up again. Her shoulder length blonde hair rested on the collar of her cream-coloured shirt as we spoke, while over her shoulder the background of our videocall revealed a neat, stylish apartment with art, indoor plants, ceramics, and books. Despite being a very high-functioning woman, the tentacles of grief were holding Samantha back.

"After five years it feels like this grief doesn't belong inside me, and I would like to get rid of it altogether if I could," she told me. "We both discussed it before he died, and he doesn't want me to live that way, either. I think with him saying that, he's given me the license to not carry it as well."

I told her I'd try my best to alleviate her sadness.

Since John's death, Samantha had heard his voice, felt his presence, and had conversations with him in her dreams where he encouraged her to move forward with her life. She had most recently felt his presence a couple of weeks prior to our sessions. "He used to be around a lot. As the years go on, I don't feel his presence as much."

I wondered whether Samantha had always been open to the idea of life after death, or if that only came after having her own experiences. My own ADCs were compelling evidence, to me, that there was life after death, which made it all the more easy to accept the phenomenon of IADC when I first learnt about it. I was curious about Samantha's earlier experiences, but I didn't want to sidetrack our first session by deviating from the protocol. Too often the first appointment can inadvertently turn into a counselling session, and I needed to avoid that at all costs. Clients feel good to be listened to in that way, but if we were going to smash this grief to smithereens, we needed to get out the power tools: bilateral stimulation. Bilateral stimulation reduces sadness, quickly, in a way talking to clients simply can't.

Samantha's prior spontaneous ADCs suggested to me she was

predisposed to having one during the course of her IADC therapy. But despite the name, IADC therapy isn't primarily about having ADCs, it is first and foremost about reducing sadness. Clients can end up without having an ADC and yet absolutely have a resolution of their grief and sadness. That's why I always downplay the importance or likelihood of ADCs, as a client's yearning or trying to force that outcome tends to inhibit it. Instead, I tell my clients that my goal is to reduce their sadness, and if an ADC occurs, that's a cherry on top. Most importantly, Samantha was open, attuned to the world around her; observant, but not judgemental. And she wasn't avoidant of her emotions. In other words, she was a prime candidate for therapy to go well.

"We have this funny joke," Samantha told me, "whenever I go to my daughter's school meetings, there's always a spare empty chair next to me that nobody ever sits in. At Emma's graduation, the same thing happened. The whole room was full and there was an empty chair next to me!"

But the most pronounced experience of John's presence to date, was the moment he died. Samantha, her daughter Emma, and John's best friend, had gone for a walk to get coffee. "While we were sitting there waiting for the coffee, I had this feeling of hot, warm energy." She started to tear up. "I could feel him. It was like he was saying goodbye. Because I could actually feel his personality. It was really weird. It was like someone standing next to you, you just feel who they are. And he said to me 'I've gone'. I just knew, and I turned to his best friend and said, 'John's gone'. But I felt that he was really happy.

"As we walked back, I knew the whole time that he wasn't going to be alive. When we got to the door the doctor came out, I said, 'Yeah I know, he's already died'. The time of death was exactly when I felt him."

We were working over Zoom; Samantha in Western Australia, and me in Adelaide. When we started the bilateral stimulation – using specific software to guide her eye movements across the computer screen – she felt her sadness lifting after the very first set. The sadness came in waves — sometimes intense — but each wave subsided quickly as we worked. Like other IADC clients, she had spontaneous insights from the processing.

"A lot of my sadness is tied up with my daughter. Maybe I don't feel strong enough sometimes to carry on by myself. And I can just see that she, forever, is missing something in her life, and it's something that I can't replace for her. She is very similar to her father, they were like two peas in a pod. I was often the one who felt left out, oddly enough. I feel like she's very lonely with him gone. She doesn't connect with me in the same way."

After one set of processing this piece of sadness, she found it hard to access it again. It was already starting to subside.

"One thing that just popped into my head is, that when John was sick and even after he died, I just became invisible. Everything became about his illness and what he wanted to do before he died, and everybody just looked at me like the carer, you know? Like I lost my whole identity. Nobody took care of me at all."

Once she felt the sadness of that piece lift, we moved on to another. This time, it was about confronting the issue of how she was treated by John. She became tearful describing how it was only after he'd died that she realised how wrong the episodes of abuse were. The tears flowed freely as Samantha stepped into the full depth of her emotions. Yet despite the intensity of each wave of emotion, the next set of eye movement would consistently reduce her distress. By the end of the first day's processing, Samantha was feeling "lighter" and "a lot less emotional".

At the beginning of the next day's session, Samantha told me she'd had her best night's sleep in years. "Ever since John died, I've never slept properly. Last night was the first time I slept the whole night without waking up!" When I asked her to reflect on the progress we'd made, and any other sadness that had come up since we spoke the previous afternoon, she had a clear answer.

"What arose after yesterday is that around John dying, actually him dying, I'm okay with that. I'm more sad about not being able to communicate with him about the things happening now, like sharing all the parenting decisions, and seeing how much of an impact his death has had on my daughter, and how hard it's made my life." She paused, then I heard the emotion returning to her voice. "And I've had a really hard life."

Samantha had overcome a dysfunctional upbringing. She was kidnapped at fifteen, was victim to a stalker, and then endured all the tumultuous times with John, including his abuse. She had risen above these obstacles to be a very successful professional, but also to maintain a kind, loving, and optimistic nature.

"It's made me realise that he was one person in a chain of a whole lot of people that have not treated me very well." She began to cry. "I carry a lot of sadness over the way he treated us. I'm a very strong person, but maybe not strong enough to walk away. My mum was in an abusive relationship like that for years, so I was taught not to have boundaries. Bad things keep happening to me, and I keep rising above it, trying to pay it forward and help other people, but no one actually helps me. That is the sadness that I carry: no one helps me." Samantha dabbed her eyes with a tissue.

We worked through sets of eye movement, and eventually Samantha declared: "The final bit for me is about my relationship with my daughter, and how hard that has been since John passed away. With him not being here, and me having to deal with everything on my own, you know? His death has caused a lot of these issues with us. It just changes the dynamic when you go from three to just two of you. It can go from really great, to awful. It's one or the other. I feel like it's a continuation of the relationship John and I had in many ways. And that's really sad."

I wanted to move straight into the bilateral stimulation while Samantha was feeling that sadness. So rather than validating how sad her situation with her daughter was, or asking her to elaborate, I wasted no time getting her eyes moving. "Okay, well, let's work on that piece, and see what happens as we go. Follow the blue ball," I said, referring to the way I administer eye movement through the video call.

Over successive sets, Samantha reported relief followed by other waves of sadness. We needed to continue until it was gone.

"With my daughter, I feel like I'm fighting her father all over again. I've contributed to this issue by not leaving, because at the time I didn't know what was happening to me. I get really sad about being on my own, and being widowed, and having to deal with all this on my own."

Anytime Samantha's emotions increased while she was talking, as they were now, I had her go straight into more eye movements. I was looking for the waves of sadness to give way to good feelings. I wasn't sure when it would happen, but I had to trust the process. In my mind's eye I would sometimes visualise icebergs melting, as if the pieces of sadness were dissolving. After two more sets, it seemed we had broken through.

"I feel heaps better," she reported.

When Samantha was unable to locate any more sadness, we went into the induction phase of IADC therapy: when the sadness is greatly reduced or not able to be felt, and the onset of good feelings occurs, this is the time a client is predisposed to having an ADC. Sometimes ADCs will spontaneously occur in this phase of the treatment, but if they don't, we give them a little prod. If an ADC occurred now, it would do something more than just further reducing her sadness, it would give Samantha an opportunity to address the unresolved issues she had with John. It was time to prod.

"What would you want to say to John if you could?" I asked.

"I think the first thing I would say is I'm sorry that we both had that experience, because it wasn't good for either of us. And I wish that I had walked away, because I needed to do that for myself, but also... for him. We could have still been successful parents together but not in the same house. I wish I could have had that conversation with him."

"So, it's going to feel very similar," I explained, as we started the second phase of the protocol. "We're going to do sets of eye movement but rather than focusing on sadness, I'm just going to get you to think about John in a general way. And now you've posed some of these things that you'd like to say, you don't need to repeat them. When you close your eyes at the end of the set, keep them closed as long as you like. As long as you're noticing something, keep your eyes closed. If nothing's happening, open them. Just go with whatever happens. It's up to you when you open them again. Follow the blue ball."

At the end of the set of eye movements, Samantha closed her eyes. At first, she looked peaceful. Then after about thirty seconds, her expression changed. She became overwhelmed with emotion. Tears emerged from her closed eyelids as she attended to her internal experience. It had worked!

"Tell me what happened there, Samantha" I asked when she opened her eyes again.

"So... I can actually feel him here," she said, waving her arm around the left side of her body as she breathed deeply through the emotion. "In his energy, he is just really sorry."

She took another breath before continuing.

"He's all here," she said waving her arms again. "It's very hot. That's how I feel. I don't know how else to describe it, and I know I sound nuts, but it's how I feel. I get very overwhelmed when he's there. All I can feel is how sorry he is… It's very overwhelming for me." Her brow furrowed; she was teetering on the edge of tears as she spoke.

"And how do you feel in response to that, that he's sorry?" I asked.

"I feel good, but I know I don't look good!" she laughed. "It feels good that he's sorry. I can really feel that he's sorry."

"Is there anything you want to say in response to this apology from him?"

"Yeah, I accept that he's sorry. And I'm sorry. Can we just leave it in the past so we can move forward now? I don't want to carry this anymore."

Another set of eye movements allowed the ADC to continue.

"What he's saying – how it feels – is that he's saying he loves me more than anything, and he wants to take that away [the burden]. So, it feels like it's going. And it just felt very light. Everything feels light, it was just going here," she said waving her hands around her.

"He wants to take the bad stuff away?" I asked.

"Yeah. He'll take it with him. I don't need it. He doesn't want me to have it. So, he's taking it."

"He's taking that baggage away and lifting it off you?"

"Yeah. I feel lighter and have started to feel more peaceful about it. I sound like a lunatic!", she laughed.

"Not at all," I smiled back. "You sound like someone who is having an after-death communication. It's pretty normal to me! I'm happy to be guided by you here, Samantha, but we talked about this present issue being the parenting on your own. There's some challenging stuff there. Is it worth putting that to John… what you're grappling with, and see what the response is?"

She agreed, and we did another set of eye movements. Samantha had her eyes closed for several minutes, with tears occasionally running down her cheeks. Then she opened her eyes to report back to me.

"We had a big conversation about that! He said she's definitely going to go to America. He said he's tried to help to make sure I have the means to get her there. He's never going to stop being her dad. He will give her a kick up the arse if she needs it. He's always going to be there and watch over her. And he's sorry that I'm having to deal with all this stuff on my own. I feel happy! I don't feel so alone in it. He's very much still her dad, is what he's telling me. He also just told me he was sending someone to me, to love, and that they're going to be fabulous. I didn't ask about that, but he's saying, 'don't worry, I've got it covered'. And the last thing he's saying is 'you're ready'. I don't know if I am, but that's what he's saying."

A serenity came over Samantha, as she relaxed her furrowed brow for the first time in two days. I was mentally drained, but I could only imagine how draining it had all been for her. She had run the emotional marathon and now stood on the other side, satisfied and free. I asked Samantha, as I do of all my clients, if she wanted any more sets of eye movement, but I was confident I knew her answer. She'd gotten what she needed out of the two sessions, she had finally released the burden of her grief.

"My heart feels really happy now," she confirmed.

I finished the therapy feeling deeply satisfied, but also in awe. Even though I'd now witnessed dozens of ADCs in my clients, it still amazed me. And, regardless of the presence of an ADC, I was amazed at how efficient IADC therapy was at processing sadness.

I sent Samantha an email a few days later, to see how she was going. This was her reply:

Hi Tom,

Thank you so much for checking in on me.

I am absolutely incredible. The treatment has worked. My sadness has gone completely. So weird and I don't miss it at all. I feel really happy and like myself again.

It is the first time in so many years there is no internal battle. I also never realised how sad I was until it was gone. It was more of a burden for me than I realised, in terms of constantly draining my energy.

I feel very optimistic about my future and the next chapter. I actually feel like I have finally moved on rather than moved forward.

Thank you for including me in the study. I am excited that other people will have the opportunity to heal in this way too.

I am very grateful! Have a lovely week.

Samantha

A few weeks later I checked in on Samantha again to see if the gains from her therapy had persisted. They had:

I am very peaceful and feeling back to myself. Had no idea how exhausting sadness actually was lol!

The treatment has been transformational for me and thanks again for including me in your study. I hope others are experiencing the same thing as I am.

It has been life changing for me.

Chapter 7

Dying is Beautiful

Being visited by my grandparents after their deaths stoked my curiosity for what happens after we die. I was sure my grandparents had lived on, but I didn't know much about the nature of their continued existence, nor the process of dying. I figured that the best way to learn about what happens after death, is to hear it from people who have died. I voraciously consumed the stories of near-death experiencers to further immerse myself in death, dying, and spirituality.

The term 'near-death experience' was coined by psychiatrist and researcher Dr Raymond Moody in his acclaimed 1975 international bestseller *Life After Life*[5]. In it, he analysed over 150 case studies of people who had experienced clinical death, been revived, and provided testimony on their experience of existing separate from their physical bodies. Dr Moody identified common qualities that represent a coherent, recognisable set of phenomena that suggest we survive bodily death:

- The sensation of being separate from one's physical body
- An overwhelming sense of peace and wellbeing
- Floating or moving through darkness or a tunnel
- Encountering a golden light

- Communicating with the light or other beings
- A review of one's life or parts of one's life
- Experiencing another world of great beauty

These phenomena consistently appear across the hundreds of NDE cases that have been documented by researchers studying NDEs across generations and cultures. They provide a compelling argument that there is a reality beyond this life, and that our physical existence is merely a temporary foray into separateness from a much more expansive, cohesive, and comforting reality.

One of the NDEs that really affected me was that of Dr. Peter Cummings, a forensic pathologist from Maine in the United States, who had a profound NDE that significantly altered his perspective on life and death. I assumed his medical and scientific training would mean he'd take a critical eye to any such experience and provide a credible account of what happened to him.

During a whitewater rafting trip in Costa Rica for his wife's 50th birthday, Cummings, who had always been apprehensive about water, found himself in a dire situation when the raft he was in flipped, and he was pulled under the water by a raging current. While underwater, Cummings was surprisingly calm despite the life-threatening situation. He vividly recalls being beside a large boulder under the water, surrounded by a peculiar movement of bubbles and a bright light. During this experience, he felt an overwhelming sense of love and heard a voice reassuring him that his family would be okay. Cummings was later able to confirm that his wife and son had indeed been rescued from the water and were safe. Cummings' Apple Watch indicated a period of approximately eight minutes during which no heart rate was recorded, suggesting a period of cardiac arrest.

After his NDE, Cummings reported experiencing a loving, peace-filled world beyond the physical, which provided a new and different perspective on his priorities. He found himself reassessing his life and career, eventually moving away from intense academic pursuits and changing how he approached his work as a pathologist, particularly in how he addressed questions about suffering and death. "I think back to all the times as a forensic pathologist I knocked on doors to tell people that loved ones were dead," he said on Sandra Champlain's *Shades of the Afterlife* podcast[6], "I brought people down into the morgue to identify bodies. I've sat with families in very horrible circumstances, and the number one question I've always been asked is: 'Did they suffer?' As a physician you always say 'No, of course not, this was sudden', and we try to comfort them. But I always felt like a liar because I don't know. Right now, I know. And I wish I could talk to those people again and say, look, this is beautiful... even under these horrible circumstances. The horrible circumstance is a second. The process after that is incredible and there's nothing to worry about in that regard." He observed, "We've made [death] so sterile and kept it behind this curtain that we don't get a chance to really experience and celebrate the transformation that is happening."

Unlike Dr Cummings, I was seeing grief at the other end, when people had been stuck and struggling with the sadness of their loss, sometimes for many years. It occurred to me that part of grief is the loss – the sense of separateness, missingness and a belief we can't get our loved one back – but another part is the bewilderment that comes from speculating about their experience. Did it hurt? Were they distressed or confused? Was their final moment consumed by feeling lost and alone? We continue to feel empathy for our loved ones after they're gone, worrying about their experience during death and even after their passing. Not knowing what happens at death causes a good deal of suffering. I also wondered about people who hold beliefs about punishment in the afterlife based on religious doctrine and dogma. Could there be a more distressing thought than your dearly departed being apprehended by dark forces, only to be tortured in eternal hell and damnation? Dr Cummings assures us that dying—even a horrible, sudden death like his rafting incident—is not distressing. I wondered if my grief clients had some of Cummings' insight into the "transformation" of death, whether it would change the way they grieved.

As I started working with IADC I noticed parallels between NDEs and my clients' experiences. They never received messages of distress. If anything, they perceived intense feelings of love, peace, and happiness. Clients often reported this as coming *from* the deceased person, or that they were experiencing what their loved one felt, in their current non-physical state. This convergence of evidence strengthened my conviction that death is not the end and suggested, while it's distressing for us to lose someone we love, we needn't be distressed on their behalf.

Other cases amazed me because they suggested some kind of spiritual intervention. Like the case of Vinnie Tolman, a twenty-something bodybuilder from Arlington, Texas, who collapsed after consuming a new workout supplement that was concentrated twenty times greater than the supplement he would normally take. Vinnie was dead so long, he was actually inside a body bag on the way to the morgue when he woke up![7]. He said, "…all of a sudden, I started to feel this warmth as if somebody shined like a really bright light or the sun came out from behind a cloud and started to warm my back. As it did, that warmth started to come over my whole being… I felt this… just tremendous unconditional love and peace and warmth, but also coolness at the same time coming over me."

Just like Dr Raymond Moody's research suggested, his NDE was replete with lights, peacefulness, love, and a freedom-filled out-of-body state. His experience was so pleasant, in fact, that he lamented his return to the physical: "Dying was awesome. Dying was easy. As soon as I relaxed into it and I embraced it, it was beautiful. It's so crazy that we put so much fear around death, because that was the best part. The hard part was coming back. To me, that was worse than death. It felt like a second death to be removed out of heaven, 'cause that's my home… I know it's my home."

I found the word 'home' to be frequently used by near-death experiencers in describing their new reality. Could it be that this earthly life is actually a journey away from our natural state of being, the place we all return to? I became a member of the International Association of Near Death Studies to learn more. IANDS is a global organisation that promotes research, education, and support regarding NDEs and related phenomena, aiming to foster global recognition of these profound experiences. Their journal and video archives provided a treasure trove of material for me to explore.

I came across a keynote presentation by Dannion Brinkley, a remarkable man who ultimately had four NDEs, from being struck by lightning and various surgeries. I had previously read his book *Saved by the Light*[8], but I'd never heard him speak. His southern drawl seemed only to add to the impact of his animated preacher-style of presenting, with passion and humour[9].

"You do not die and there is no hell!" Dannion proclaimed as if standing at a pulpit. "When your time comes, you're going to be so happy, you're not going to know what to do with yourself. You'll know that space and place [the afterlife] more than you've ever known any place on this Earth."

Dannion went on to describe the process of death. I figured he was as qualified as anyone to talk about death.

"Imagine that you're six years old and it's Christmas. And you're going to your grandmothers. And she's rich. And you're her favourite child. She lives in Anaheim. And her last name is Disney. And you come to the stoplight. When that stop light goes from red to green, you turn left, you turn right, and you pull up and there's Grandma and Mickey waiting up. Now how scared of that can you be?!" he bellowed. "How frightened can you be of that? And you have been taught to be terrified. Get over it! It ain't gonna happen. It ain't scary."

Dannion Brinkley's extensive forays into the afterlife have provided him with rich insights not just into death, but what death teaches us about the purpose of life. You'll hear more about Dannion's insights in Chapter 17.

I found the Near Death Experience Research Foundation (nderf.org), the amazing research archive of Dr Jeff and Judy Long in which they catalogue thousands of self-reported NDEs, and consumed these accounts voraciously. I learned that not only do near-death experiencers frequently refer to feeling no pain, but they also experience a complete restoration of any lost faculties (such as sight) or disabilities.

The restorative and healing nature of the afterlife is described by Bollette, a Danish mother, who reported an NDE during the birth of her tenth child, during which she learned that "to die is so amazingly beautiful and full of joy and love. I felt myself to be very awake and aware the whole time... I felt more fresh and energised than ever, much more than when I am in life... I was energized, joyful and curious. I was there in the present moment, totally in the present. I felt no pain or gave it any thought."[10]

These accounts from NDEs are remarkably consistent with the perceptions of those who experience ADCs, who also often describe that the deceased eventually seem to return to their healthy, youthful selves, or the time in which they felt the happiest, as with my Nanna.

The tunnel and lights, as catalogued by Dr Raymond Moody, appeared repeatedly too, as in the case of Will S who was in surgery having a benign tumour removed from his back when he had an allergic reaction to the anaesthesia: "The light had gorgeous golden, almost yellow, tendrils swirling around it. The colour at its core was pure white. As the light hovered in front of me, I could hear a high-pitched ringing sound. I experienced the most profoundly overwhelming, astonishing, indescribable feelings of unconditional love, peace, joy, understanding, and acceptance."[11]

My research participant Susanne had reported a purple light and a white orb in her ADC. In fact, seeing colours is a common precursor to the onset of an ADC. This was yet another similarity between ADCs and NDEs.

And just like IADC therapy, NDEs involve the reunion, or reconnection, of the experiencer with their deceased loved ones. Karen Thomas had an NDE during surgery in which she was reunited with "…my father, who had died when I was seven, and my brother, who had been killed in a car accident, and aunts and uncles that I knew had passed away. Then there were four other people, beings, that were there who I just knew. I had never seen pictures of my grandparents because they had died before I was born, long before I was born, but yet I knew that that's who they were. And it was like a huge family reunion."[12]

These reunion experiences particularly resonated with my IADC work. Just as near-death experiencers report joyful reunions with deceased loved ones, my clients often experience similar moments of reconnection during therapy. The consistency of these experiences across different contexts – NDEs, spontaneous ADCs, and IADC therapy – suggests something profound about the nature of consciousness and our bonds with loved ones. NDE accounts are overwhelmingly positive experiences, reflecting extraordinary happiness, love, and peace, despite the outward physical calamity that death appears to be. My IADC clients reported intense peace, love, and positive emotions despite the proximity and depth of their presenting despair. And Nanna, Grandpa, and Nanny all radiated immense peace, happiness, and love directly to me. I couldn't ignore these patterns and the suggestion that all these experiences are tapping into a beautiful reality for those on the other side.

These stories are not the exception. They are simply eloquent, descriptive testimonies of the consistent themes identified in a growing body of NDE research. Eminent researchers such as Professor Jan Holden and Professor Bruce Greyson, recognised pioneers in the scientific study of NDEs, compiled volumes of evidence to further our understanding of these phenomena. The more I consumed NDE stories and the opinions of scientific researchers, the more confident I became in nine clear truths:

1. Contrary to our greatest fears, those who die do not cease to exist.

2. Dying is generally not distressing, and is usually profoundly peaceful, calming, healing, and defined by an all-encompassing sense of being loved and protected. In other words, dying is beautiful.

3. The pain and distress we imagine our loved one's suffering – especially when dying from accidents or assaults – isn't commonly reported. Instead, NDE testimony suggests many people leave their bodies *before* their body has suffered the impact which causes death.

4. People generally do not regret being 'dead', in fact they report a greater sense of connectedness with all things and a more complete and expansive awareness, including knowledge of the universe and how it functions.

5. Their personalities continue.

6. They live a much broader, freer existence, unencumbered by the limitations of our physical reality.

7. They are healed and returned to health and wholeness. Those who suffered from illness, disability and/or chronic pain are restored and enjoy an ongoing sense of lightness and wellbeing.
8. When glimpsing the other side, they often feel so good they don't want to return.
9. Our bonds are not broken by death. We can perceive these connections through after-death communications, and we will be reunited with our loved ones after we die.

As both a clinician and someone who has experienced ADCs firsthand, these accounts transformed my understanding of death and grief. When clients come to me fearing for their deceased loved ones' wellbeing, I can now share with confidence that death, while challenging for us who remain, appears to be a peaceful transition for those who experience it. The 'deceased' don't cease to exist at all. And the maxim that "they are in a better place" is entirely correct. These realisations also give us clues for how to adapt through the emotional burdens of grief:

1. Acknowledge your loved one continues.
2. You can maintain ongoing bonds with the person who passed over.
3. The greater your appreciation of this non-physical, spiritual life, the closer you will feel to him or her.

If you are grieving, I offer this assurance: your sadness, when someone you love has died, is completely understandable. Your loss of that dear person in this physical life may well be devastating to you. But do not be afraid or saddened *for them*. For those who die, dying is beautiful. More love and peace than they have ever known on this Earth awaits them. They will continue, and they will be fine. And so will each of us. So to those who are afraid of death: do not be afraid of death, any more than you would be afraid of birth. Death is a transition. Merely a doorway from this world to the next, which is our true home.

Chapter 8

Arianne

Life was going well for Arianne when one Saturday morning she walked into the bedroom to find her fiancé, Hugo, on the floor after he'd suffered a massive stroke.

"Initially, I thought he was being stupid, because he would just do silly random things. But as soon as I clocked his eyes, I knew something really bad had happened," Arianne told me through tears on our Zoom call. "He had his eyes open, and he could move one side of his body, but he wasn't *there.*"

Hugo died three days later. And Arianne's life as she knew it, ended.

I asked Arianne how she would describe Hugo's personality, and their relationship.

"He was cheeky, caring, silly, full of life... and incredibly intense," she said. "We had a really beautiful relationship. The big complication with his death is that I had a difficult childhood, and Hugo was my first experience of safety and love. Like real, unconditional, true love – and I didn't realise this until he died."

Their relationship still had its challenges. Hugo had a son from a previous relationship, and they shared parenting with Hugo's ex-wife.

"We were both coming from families of loss and working together to try to work that out. I feel like we just started to find our groove when he died. That was really cruel." As Arianne described her heartbreak, I could feel my eyes stinging. When a person dies naturally after a full life – like Nanna in her nursing home at age 84 – you can be sad, but you can't complain about it being tragic. But so many of my IADC clients were people who had lost loved ones in the prime of their lives, and these always drew me in emotionally. I guess that's why I was drawn to being a psychologist in the first place, I had a natural empathy for others. But I couldn't let it overwhelm me. I had to stay focused.

Arianne revealed another aspect of why this was so painful: it turned out she wasn't just dealing with the immense loss of her true love and all their future plans, she also carried a hidden burden: guilt. The morning she found Hugo on the floor, they had slept in separate bedrooms. It was something they would occasionally do because of his snoring. She had no reason to suspect anything was wrong, she was just letting him have a sleep-in. When Arianne walked in to find him at around 10 a.m., he was alive, but cold.

"I feel really responsible for him." Arianne was sobbing now. "And like I left it too late. In some ways I feel as though I killed him. I know that sounds insane but that's how it feels. Because I wasn't there soon enough." Arianne took a few breaths to compose herself.

Because Hugo was an organ donor, he was kept on life support for three days, allowing Arianne to sleep in the hospital bed with him for two nights. It was on the second night that she felt him 'leave'.

"I felt really safe and happy and contained in the world with him in it. And I've not felt that since he's gone." At this point I could see Arianne was really accessing her sadness. When recounting her love for Hugo, Arianne's face would light up, her wavy brown hair framing a beautiful smile; but now she was overcome with emotion, her shoulders slumped forward as if defeated, revealing a bookshelf and bright orange Aboriginal artwork behind her. Now was the time to start processing. I had her start alternately tapping her shoulders with the butterfly hug technique.

IADC therapy works by implementing bilateral stimulation *while* the client is experiencing very intense sadness, so even though Arianne was in the middle of crying, I didn't want to help her settle or wait until her emotions calmed. Instead, I instructed her to tap as she was crying. The most painful part of her experience, at that very moment, was the belief that she had let Hugo down, and how much she misses him. She felt she was "clinging to him."

After the very first set she said the image of Hugo lying on the floor was "dissolving". This is a common sign that the bilateral stimulation is working to process highly emotional and distressing images. She initially spoke with her eyes still closed: "I don't know how to describe it, but I get this feeling of *'don't personalise this'*."

Over the coming several sets of tapping, following her strongest 'pieces' of sadness, Arianne described the intensity as moving in waves. Most importantly, Arianne was open to whatever she may experience, she trusted the process and was completely open to the full intensity of her emotions. This was crucial for the IADC protocol to be as effective as possible. If she wasn't willing to step into the full burn of her sadness and grief, it would impede the process. Like peeling back layers, the waves rose and fell as we followed wherever the strongest sadness appeared.

"You're doing great, keep tapping," I encouraged as she commenced another set, and the tears flowed again. After each set, I would ask Arianne what she noticed about her sadness. She said her sadness was starting to "soften", but there were more pieces for us to confront. "I feel sad for myself, I guess. For beating myself up for all of this. Because of the breakdown of everything... I've been punishing myself."

"Let's go with that, that's a new piece," I said, and prompted her to commence yet another set of tapping. After further sets, Arianne said her strongest sadness was simply the loss of companionship. She'd had a beautiful, comforting, secure relationship, and it ended in the blink of an eye. As we processed it, an ADC began to unfold.

"Halfway through I started to feel Hugo. I'm laughing because it's like I can hear him saying 'What are you doing girl? You've completely and utterly exhausted yourself!'. I can feel him say 'Let it go'. The reason I haven't felt him closer to me before now is because of all the shame and guilt that I have, and that I'm not leaning in to him." She kept her eyes closed as she spoke, relaying her experience to me while also attending to the ongoing connection. I whispered so as not to interrupt her focus.

"The shame and the guilt were blocking it?" I asked softly.

"Yes. It's like I can't face him because of what I did to him. He's there saying: 'You didn't do this to me. Let me help you on this next phase.'"

I wanted to know what Arianne was feeling emotionally. An ADC is usually accompanied by strong, positive emotions. "What are you feeling emotionally when you feel that connection with Hugo?"

"It feels really peaceful. And I think when I connect with him I get sad because it reminds me of him physically being here. Like I can't deal with that, so I block him, and I don't want to block him." Although Arianne was experiencing an ADC – she spontaneously reported she was perceiving Hugo's presence during the processing – there was a piece of sadness that came along with that. To help strengthen her experience, we needed to immediately step into that. Because the ADC had started and was likely to unfold further, we needed to shift gears a little.

"Just let yourself feel that," I told Arianne, keeping the momentum going. "I want you to start tapping, but when I tell you to stop, just keep your eyes closed for as long as you're noticing anything, okay? And I'll leave it to you when you're ready to let me know what's happening, and whenever you want to open your eyes, okay? As long as you're noticing anything you can keep your eyes closed for as long as you want." Arianne nodded and restarted the rhythmic tapping of her shoulders.

I said, "stop", almost whispering, when the time was right.

With her eyes closed, Arianne cried intensely for a few moments, then sighed peacefully, and remained quiet for several minutes. I watched her facial expression soften as she inhaled deeply, as the tears made their way down her cheek to her chin and into her lap below. There was a peacefulness about her expression. Her brow softened. She swayed ever so gently as she attended to her internal experience, sitting quietly for several more minutes. After about ten minutes of silence, she smiled, almost suppressing a laugh. And then opened her eyes.

"What did you notice?", I asked.

"I noticed in the beginning that instead of wanting him here that I really wanted to be with him. I could feel Hugo come in and he's telling me in his cheeky way... he's saying 'even if you come here, which you will in due time, it's not going to be the same'. It won't be 'Arianne and Hugo' going on as 'Arianne and Hugo' as it was on Earth. He's saying no, that isn't how it works.

"It's like he is trying to help me release this.. um.. clutching, this desire for either him to be here or me to be there. It's like he's helping me and he's telling me what it is I need to focus on, and what it is I need to do." Still with her eyes closed, Arianne laughed. "I kept getting this visual... whenever he wanted to have a serious chat, he would put his undies on his head. I'm getting this image of him with his undies on his head which I know is code for: 'I'm having a serious conversation with you!' It's like he's saying, 'you've got shit to do here, and you need to do it, and I'm here to be your guide.'"

For the first time since Hugo's death, Arianne felt like she was meant to be here. She could finally let go of the yearning for his physical presence, or the desire to be with him. She had a purpose, a reason for living, and Hugo was going to help her move forward.

"It's like him dying is all part of a bigger plan." She went on to paraphrase the messages she was getting in her ADC. "Don't think of yourself as an individual and don't think of us as individuals. We're all part of one web of consciousness. And basically, we all have a role within this consciousness to play. He's saying there's a bigger, higher purpose to it all. He's saying: 'your whole life, everything that you've been through, is here for a reason. And your time to shine and step into all of that, is now.'"

Arianne finished the first day's session feeling exhausted but relieved. She was finally able to let go of the longing she had, to either be with him, or have their relationship somehow restored to what it used to be.

The following afternoon we resumed our therapy over Zoom. My first task was to check in on how Arianne was feeling. IADC therapy can be exhausting for clients, and it can also cause new pieces of sadness to arise, as if those pieces dissolved on day one have made room for other pieces to rise to the surface. Dr Botkin used the metaphor of whack-a-mole to describe the relentless task IADC Therapists and clients have to processes sadness as it arises over the two days of the protocol. Arianne said she was feeling much better but the night before had felt like she'd run a marathon. I also wanted to check on her level of sadness right now.

"It's about a five," she said referring to the ten-point scale we use to rate intensity of sadness. Then, we began the processing.

"Really quickly I could feel Hugo come in. It's like he's coaching me. Again, the message is 'Let it go. You don't have to carry it.'" After another set, Arianne easily resumed the ADC and was quiet for several minutes, until she opened her eyes.

"This is getting really intense. What happened is: Hugo was there, then he said 'I've got your Pop here' (my Mum's dad), and then it's like… I could feel him… and what he said to me is 'don't worry I've got your mum.' He's giving me permission to not feel so responsible for my mum, who is alive.

"Then what came through was… my dad had a sister who drowned when she was five… she came through and she wanted to tell me that he feels responsible for her death because she drowned in the river. Then I could feel my great-grandmother, my nan's mum. Recently I had this conversation with my nan about her mother, and what she had endured with the death of her little sister. She's coming through with a different energy and she's lighter and says, 'thank you'. It's like all these messages coming through."

I was keen for this experience to not overwhelm Arianne. It's not uncommon for clients to report the presence of more than one person in their ADC, but this sounded like a lot. If Hugo was her strongest connection, she could ask him what he wanted to share with her, without everyone connecting with her at once. Arianne agreed to give it a try. We did another set, and she reported back to me with a softer, calmer voice once she opened her eyes.

"At the moment it's like he's being very pushy but not in a negative sense. It's kind of how he was when he was alive. He said, 'now is the time to act'. He's trying to give me permission to be in a relationship with another man and not have to worry about all this guilt about him. He's saying, 'I'm proud of you for letting go of the fantasy of you and I forever and ever, because that's not how it works'. I'm feeling this real lightness between Hugo and I right now."

It was hard to believe that we'd only done three sets of bilateral stimulation and already Arianne was in an ADC state that was not fragile in any way. She could alternately speak with me, reflect on what she was experiencing, and then go directly back into her communication with Hugo. Arianne lent back in her chair, relaxing into what was happening, absorbing it.

"It's this really beautiful feeling. He just wants to tell me 'I love you and I'm so proud of you.' It feels like the slate is clean… finally. It feels really good! I've had this constant urge to try and resolve things. It feels very much like finally the past has happened. It's like I'm now able to meet him where he's at and let us go. It feels really weird because I was on this perpetual search."

All up, her ADC with Hugo lasted over half an hour.

Arianne had just had an extraordinary experience, yet somehow, she was able to articulate everything so clearly. It occurred to me that she was a very psychologically minded client; rather than being overwhelmed, she was curious and brought a genuine openness to the experience. She offered the following reflection at the end:

"I'm comparing this experience to other therapies that have really worked for me, and the difference is that a lot more was able to be covered and resolved really quickly with IADC therapy. I feel like it's done. There's nothing else to search for. The book has closed now. I've not experienced that in a therapeutic exchange before, which is why I'm spinning out. This process is not what I was expecting. I didn't think it was going to be so effective."

ADCs can be quick and subtle, or elaborate and intense. For whatever reason, Arianne's ADC was not a fleeting moment of connection, but more like a prolonged, in-depth phone conversation with many people getting in on the call. The bilateral stimulation had reduced her sadness significantly, and her ADC had yielded insights that were, therapeutically speaking, a quantum leap forward in her grieving process.

A month later, I caught up with Arianne to debrief. I wanted to see how she was going and also get any feedback she might have on the therapy. In her typically self-aware manner, she gave me some very useful insights.

"IADC deals with mind, body and spirit," she said. "Because you're dealing with the sadness (the emotions), then you're using the body to process the emotions (the tapping)... and the spirit part..." She paused. "The biggest thing I noticed was while you had questions, there was this allowance of space. And that's where the spirit – the non-physical world – interacts with us, and where the magic happens, when you allow that process."

Arianne had nailed it. Unlike talk therapies, CBT, counselling, Acceptance and Commitment Therapy, and others, IADC therapy does something completely different. Thoughts and words are merely tools of communication, nothing more. Instead of thoughts and words constructing the substance of the therapy, we create a space where emotions are brought forward and processed, the thinking brain is quietened, and when good feelings come in, we allow the time and space for beautiful things to unfold. It is in this sacred space that peace, happiness, and the presence of loved ones can naturally occur. We don't force it, we don't analyse it, and we don't worry about what beliefs you have or don't have. The result is a very natural, personal, spiritual, and psychological resolution.

"I think it's a really powerful and effective therapy... so fast!" Arianne continued. What she liked about IADC was how direct it was. Her experience of traditional counselling was that it's possible to spend a lot of time on peripheral issues. I believe this is one of the key reasons why IADC therapy can be effective when traditional grief counselling sometimes is not. Psychotherapy and counselling can be complicit in prolonging distress because it skirts around it. It's all about 'How can we manage your feelings?' rather than 'How can we process them?'. That's why progress with IADC therapy is so fast. It goes direct to the core and processes the sadness associated with a loss.

"It really helped me to have a deep resolution with his death and the circumstances surrounding his death, which was huge. Because there was so much guilt and angst around that which was keeping me paralysed. And I'm not lying when I say: afterwards it hasn't bothered me."

I felt a tingle all over when Arianne said that. *This* is what I'd been missing all those years when I'd scurry away from grief clients like a wimp walking away from a fight. That's why I was doing this research study, why I was happily giving up my nights and weekends collecting research data. To have this amazing tool made *me* feel amazing. Therapists want to heal; they get a buzz from helping people get better. Finally, I was able to help people get better even when they'd been through the worst experience of their lives. I wasn't afraid of the fight anymore!

And to top it all off, Arianne also mentioned that she had further experiences of Hugo's presence since our sessions. "One of the biggest gifts to come out of this is: I feel like I have the most intimate relationship with Hugo that I've ever had. Which is so weird to say! It's like I know him on such a deeper level."

"It has been such a huge gift," Arianne continued. "I can see so clearly in hindsight had I not done this therapy with you that I would still be in the same boat, and I would still be doing the counselling that I've been doing... but you go right to the core issue, and you deal with it, and you allow it. There's nothing else out there that does that. It's hugely powerful, so I feel really grateful for this. It's helped me to come home to myself, and be free, and feel like I can start life over.

"That's a gift. So, thank you, Tom."

Chapter 9

Reasons to Be Alive

When people return from near-death experiences, something fascinating happens. Their reactions split into two distinct paths. Some, overwhelmed by memories of the love and peace they experienced, find themselves longing for 'home' – that remarkable realm of light and connection they glimpsed on the other side. The physical world feels dense, heavy, almost unbearable in comparison. For some, it becomes a kind of adjustment disorder, and they are prone to depression. And honestly, who could blame them? After experiencing that profound love and peace, this earthly existence must feel like a poor substitute. But others return with an entirely different response: they embrace life with renewed vigour, dedicating themselves to helping others, pursuing spiritual growth, and living with profound purpose. Same experience, dramatically different outcomes.

Professor Jan Holden's research at the University of North Texas reveals that this divergence isn't random. Those who 'integrate' their experience – who understand that our physical life serves a vital purpose in our soul's multidimensional journey – tend to live more meaningful, purposeful lives after their NDE. They become less materialistic, more spiritually attuned, and often dedicate themselves to service[13].

This pattern raises a crucial question: If the other side is so wonderful – so full of love, peace and connection – why are we here at all? And more importantly, why should we stay when life becomes difficult? And for the grieving person who may be longing to be with their deceased loved one on the other side, what's keeping them here? These are serious questions that naturally arise when you consider all the stories of how amazing, loving, and peaceful the other side is. Being in this physical life is tough. It can be wonderful, for sure. But at some point – as I would eventually find out after years of devil-may-care attitudes toward driving, partying, and bachelorhood – somewhere along the way, it's gonna get tough. Even if you do everything right. (I didn't).

Both near-death experiencers and those in grief face the challenge of integrating their loss. Grieving people often feel traumatised, lost, and alone, grappling with the gaping absence of someone they deeply loved. This profound longing for connection mirrors the yearning near-death experiencers feel when they long for the realm of unconditional love and peace on the other side.

Just as some near-death experiencers struggle to reconcile the beauty of the afterlife with the weight of earthly life, grieving people face the task of somehow coping with the stark reality they now find themselves in, compared to the love, comfort, and peace of their relationship with the person who died. Each can be equally disorienting. Each group struggles with the persistent fleeting sense of the other side, a yearning for a love that exists across the veil, something that represented home. The absence of this love and security can feel unbearable, and life may seem hollow or even pointless in comparison. However, the lessons learned from those who integrate their NDEs offer a powerful message of hope for those in grief.

First, we can recognise that the connection endures. NDE research repeatedly shows that love transcends the boundaries of physical existence. Many experiencers return with the profound understanding that they are never truly separated from their loved ones or from the divine whole of which we are all a part. Likewise, those who have ADCs – a significant proportion of the population – experience a sense of reconnection with their loved ones, usually with commensurate love, peace, and reassurance. Even without an ADC experience, contemporary grief theories tell us that a sense of continuing bonds, whether through engaging in rituals, embracing cherished practices, or simply talking to a loved one who has passed, helps to adjust and integrate the loss into their ongoing physical life. My mum isn't yet convinced about ADCs and the afterlife, but after Grandpa died, she would often speak to him out loud. It brought her comfort and helped her to cope. I believe we are spiritual beings, whether on this side or the next, and our connections endure.

Second, it is possible to reframe life's purpose. Both near death experiencers and grieving people can find healing by contextualising their pain as a part of their larger journey. Many of my ADC clients have told me, "I now feel that everything has happened for a reason." They feel more accepting. Even amidst the pain of loss, they connect with feelings of peace and love. Those who integrate their NDEs often come to understand that physical life serves a vital purpose: to grow, love, and learn. For those in grief, integration can be found through honouring their loved one by living a meaningful life, helping others, or creating beauty in the world as a legacy to the person who died.

When counsellors and mental health or medical professionals affirm the NDE experience as valid, it is predictive of better outcomes for the experiencer[14]. I believe we should approach ADCs in the same way. For too long, people have hidden their incredible, healing experiences of reconnection out of public view. The more we acknowledge the sheer prevalence of spontaneous ADCs, and the more IADC therapy rises into view of the public consciousness, we can bring these healing experiences out into the light of day and provide better outcomes for grieving people worldwide.

My IADC clients were consistently more accepting of the death – not approving but accepting – and were able to hold a sense of deep peace in such close proximity to the distressing reality of their loss. This integration of the death occurred when they experienced peace and acceptance as an immediate consequence of stepping into the pain of that loss. It seems paradoxical, but relief from stepping into pain is the mode of action underpinning IADC. They also interpreted their experience of loss, and therapy, within a broader spiritual, philosophical, or psychological framework. They relished new insights, changing images and memories, emotions that rise and fall as a natural result of their brain's healing power being activated. Like a river winding its way to the sea, IADC guides clients to a natural healing destination, inevitably getting what they need, and their future life takes on greater significance.

Most importantly, they move forward. In preparing to publish this book, I contacted clients many months after their sessions with me. If they'd fallen back in a hole, they could tell me to go jump in the lake. Instead, they reported stories of moving forward – not necessarily moving 'on' from the people who died – but taking those cherished souls *with them* through their ongoing bonds, as they pursued new relationships, new directions, and found courage to embrace a new and different life. Ultimately, their integration of loss meant that they were no longer stuck in intense sadness and longing but living with hope and a desire to carry on. Some clients were less sad but found the removal of intense core sadness had revealed subsequent challenges: how do I find my new purpose with my loved one gone? In some circumstances a third session was requested to seek out additional gains and to strengthen continuing bonds.

I wonder about the long-term consequences of continuing bonds. Do ADCs make the experiencer more altruistic, less ego-driven, or better connected to a higher power, as near-death experiencers report? Some of this research has begun, but only time will tell. At least for now, we have direct testimony from clients themselves which is compelling data:

> "After IADC therapy, the attachment to needing my loved one in the physical was released… I feel the closest to my loved one than I ever have post-IADC and I have a renewed relationship around [their] death, with myself, and death generally."

> "I feel a strong sense of lightness, feeling calmer in my body, mind, and soul. I feel the presence of my [loved one] around me and trust in the experience that [they are] close."

> "It helped me feel a greater connection to myself as well. After IADC therapy, I have experienced more ADC experiences… They have been deeply comforting and provided me guidance."

> "Bittersweet, renewed sense that I can do this, can't wait to see [my loved one] in the afterlife but I've got things to do first."

> "I feel lighter and more positive about my future, with a knowledge that it does not decrease my love for or from [my loved one]."

> "There's something else out there. There is a 'heaven' or other dimension."

> "I feel more connected and more hopeful about how to move forward with that sense of connection to help me."

"I felt the sadness leaving me each time we found something. I feel so much lighter and happier and have a positive feeling about the future."

But what about the grieving person who doesn't integrate their loss in such a way as to find peace and move forward? Perhaps they don't believe ongoing bonds are possible, maybe they don't even know IADC therapy exists. Perhaps they are so stuck in sadness that it has become the defining theme of their life, and the overriding tenor of their waking reality. These cases are known as 'prolonged' or 'complicated' grief, mostly defined – in diagnostic terms – by the length of time in which the sufferer continues to be deeply affected by their grief 'symptoms'. Don't be put off by the language – diagnostic systems, by definition, seek to pathologise human experiences. This is for the purpose of creating a shared language, an understanding between medical and mental health professionals so we can agree on definitions and terms. But grief is a natural human reaction to loss. Whatever arbitrary dimensions are applied to it, some people struggle with grief for a long time, and their quality of life suffers. Like the near-death experiencers who suffered as a result of their unintegrated experiences, prolonged grief is the long-term manifestation of not being able to adjust to the loss and move forward. It isn't a failure of character, it is simply a very common human vulnerability and struggle.

Both prolonged grief and unintegrated NDEs are defined by a 'stuckness', an inability to move forward, a lack of direct meaning and purpose from this momentous event, with which to pursue or continue a fully functioning life. Our Adelaide University research specifically wanted to assess whether we could treat prolonged grief disorder in just two sessions with the IADC therapy protocol (I'll share the results later in this book). IADC therapy facilitates and accelerates the adjustment tasks grieving people face, it can quickly help people to accept the loss, make meaning from it in a personal and relevant way, and help them to move forward with the subsequent challenge of coping, if not thriving, in their new reality.

There are many reasons to stay engaged with life. When I was fifteen, I read a book that changed my outlook on life. *Stephen Lives: His life, suicide, and afterlife* by Anne Puryear[15], is the story of Stephen Christopher Dennis. He was also fifteen when he died by suicide. His depressed mood, humiliation after being caught shoplifting while trying desperately to fit in with other kids, and rejection by a girl he loved, all combined to result in the impulsive decision to hang himself. Stephen's mother, Anne, wrote the book to detail her experiences of communication with him from the other side.

Like a majority of NDE reports, Stephen described a life review that exposed the consequences of his actions. A life review is not a judgement – there is no external presence that judges your life as your review it – but rather we tend to judge ourselves. Stephen got a unique perspective on his influence: the effects of his decisions and interactions with others, from the other person's point of view. He felt the emotions of the people he hurt – or comforted – in his life, reliving the other person's experience. He also saw the ripple effect of his decisions. For any of us, this could be painful, but it could also be deeply satisfying and surprising.

Stephen remarked how seemingly inconsequential things mattered, that we are always influencing others even when not aware of it, and the smallest things can have the most significant impact. Although his life review revealed the terrible ripple effect of his final act, which he deeply regretted, his story showed that the flipside of recognising how far hurt can travel is that we have an equally powerful opportunity to make a positive influence in the lives of others. The message that stuck with me was: **you matter, and your presence makes a difference, even if you can't see it right now.**

Stephen lamented his lost opportunity to be a positive influence, what he calls being "a bearer of light": "It doesn't matter if it's being a teacher, cleaning streets, or being president. Your obligation is to use your gift in the very best way, to help you become the very best whole person you can, and to help others at every opportunity."

This is entirely consistent with the underpinning theme I noticed in other people's life reviews, that the purpose of life is to be of loving assistance to others. Many near-death experiencers express surprise at how the smallest acts of kindness impacted others in ways they never realised. They saw how treating others with love, dignity, and respect reverberated throughout the lives of those who received it. Whether struggling with grief, or some other problem, **we can always find purpose in helping others.** You don't need to do anything big or impressive. You just need to act out of love. To be of assistance to others in some way, any way.

It follows from this truth that when *you* need help, you are not a burden but a gift-giver. **Your needs are an opportunity for others to show love and compassion.** To be a helper, there must be someone to be helped. We each play many roles in our lives: sometimes strong and brave, other times needy and helpless. One day the protector, next the protected. In times of need, you are providing the opportunity for someone else to express their love. Allowing yourself to be helped is literally giving the gift of a beautiful moment in your helper's life review. This is the yin and the yang of all existence, and we each must take our turns. For many people their chance to help provides their greatest fulfilment. Teachers need someone to teach, nurses need someone to nurse... there are people all around you, whether professionals or friends or volunteers, who would be delighted to be a helper to you. Allow them to be a bearer of light.

It takes courage to admit vulnerability. In the eyes of the other side, **asking for help is a sign of strength, not weakness**. I believe free will is the heart of the human experience because in heaven, we are already connected and one with everything. On Earth, we are made to feel separate, to experience ourselves as if we are outside of God. Our perceived separation gives us the opportunity to cultivate love when we don't always feel surrounded by love, and this helps us evolve spiritually. But the law of free will means we must ask. So many grief clients told me they felt well supported soon after the death, only to feel that support fade as the months passed by. The initial shock had worn off, but they still had the difficult long-term task of finding their feet in their new world without the person who died. If you're grieving right now and you need help and support, please ask for it. Ask your family, ask your friends, ask your doctor or IADC therapist, call a helpline, or whoever you need to speak to. Just as spiritual progress can be achieved through courageous action in other areas of life, asking for help is no less worthy an opportunity for growth.

And always remember, **being compassionate includes self-compassion**. If the ultimate truth is that we are all one, then self-kindness is kindness to all. Treating yourself with kindness and compassion is to act with the kind of loving intent NDEs tell us we must hold in our hearts. Self-compassion invites us to acknowledge our common humanity: to be human is to be imperfect, and to sometimes need help. No matter how together your most admired role model seems, there are times they have felt frightened and feeble, and every person on this planet, regardless of their achievements and good deeds, would be ashamed of their worst moments. We are vulnerable by nature, and that means we must seek help when we need it. What can you do to be kind to yourself today?

Life is precious. Even in the midst of the hardest of hard times, it remains precious. The more I consumed stories of ADCs, NDEs, and all sorts of spiritual experiences, the clearer it became: the gift of life is our opportunity to grow as a *soul*, and we can't grow without obstacles. That's why we have this physical life. We are provided with the temporary illusion of separateness, which is our time on the stage of physical existence, playing various roles to benefit our own growth and that of others.

I accept that we cannot always see our obstacles as gifts, or our losses as tasks of spiritual evolution. But that doesn't change the reality that our very reason for being here is predicated on our free will, and our sense of separateness from others and the divine. In heaven, thought is the same as action. NDE testimony, messages from ADCs, and other spiritual texts and communications suggest the heavenly world is without fear, suffering, or separation.

When Australian Thomas Perry found himself out of body after a heart attack and panicked at the thought of leaving his children – torn between the paradise he found himself in and his responsibilities on Earth – angelic beings immediately intervened to calm him, as if negative emotions were incongruent, almost a pollutant, within that heavenly space[16]. Likewise, ADCs occur when the client is calm, relaxed, peaceful. This spiritual attunement demarcates the dense, emotional challenges of this physical life in which we forge our character, build the quality of our spirits, precisely because we do not have our every need met, with comfort, companionship, immersed in an endless sea of love. Our task in this physical life is to use our choice, our will, to live as best we can even though it can be scary and we don't have total control. Life can contain terrible suffering. But as long as we're alive, the possibility for transformation remains. Our physical life is the gift that makes growth possible.

It was a sunny morning in 2016 when, while walking my miniature schnauzer Rupert around my suburb in the Adelaide Hills, I first heard of Dr Allan Botkin. I was listening to one of my favourite podcasts, *We Don't Die Radio* with Sandra Champlain. She was interviewing Dr Botkin about his incredible therapy, Induced After Death Communication, in which his adapted EMDR protocol would rapidly reduce the sadness associated with grief, and even allow mourners to experience the presence of their deceased loved one.

I was intrigued. Could this really be true? If it was, it was right at the nexus of two of my main interests, psychology and spirituality. I ordered Dr Botkin's book immediately, devouring it during my subsequent airplane trips interstate for work. It sounded amazing, and absolutely the kind of thing I would love to do. But I was stuck.

Immersed in 50+ hour work weeks, my wife Annabel and I had a baby on the way, and I couldn't imagine when or where I could possibly start to pursue this let alone make it a professional focus. It would have to wait, I concluded. And although I convinced myself I wasn't really concerned about the reaction of friends and professional colleagues, deep down the 'woo-woo factor' did play on my mind. Little did I know then how the spectre of possible grief, and desperate appeals to those in spirit, would soon loom large in my own life.

The sun shone down on us that carefree morning. Rupert meandering to sniff all the interesting smells on the footpaths and trees, and me uplifted and excited by what I was hearing in the podcast interview. There was not a hint in my awareness that in just a matter of months my entire world would come crashing down.

Chapter 10

Sheena

Sheena approached me to be part of my University of Adelaide research study because she was grieving the loss of her 29-year-old son Chris, who had died ten years earlier. Originally from Scotland, Sheena was a trained nurse who had worked in mental health settings. She emigrated to Australia – where her daughter was living – and started a new life a couple of years after Chris died.

With long brown hair and round glasses, she told me over our Zoom call of her deep love for her son and their close bond. From what I'd gathered in our screening call about six weeks earlier, I knew there was a lot of trauma and stress leading up to Chris' death. And the pain was still evident ten years on. Intense enough that she acknowledged having to sometimes block or mask her emotions to cope.

"I find your study very interesting. That's why I've asked to be part of it," she explained. "I suppose my worry is because I'm so used to not allowing myself to go there, I do block things off. Hopefully, I'll be able to, you know, kind of let that barrier down."

Sheena's reticence to "go there" was understandable. Chris's death was the most painful experience of her life, and it is only natural to try to avoid pain. Avoidance coping is a common psychological strategy, but to resolve their distress, clients must ultimately confront the cause of their distress. Because I needed Sheena to access her sadness in order to process it, her willingness to go there was essential. But I also didn't want her to anticipate this with fear. If I followed the IADC protocol correctly, the intensity of her sadness would soon come down, and I needed her to relax into the experience as much as possible. "Let's try not to put pressure on anything. Let's just see what happens. We'll just see how it goes," I reassured her.

The other thing I needed to be sure of was that Sheena would be okay with feeling less sad. Strangely enough, many grief clients feel ambivalent about letting go of sadness. On one hand, Sheena wanted to be rid of the painful emotions that were enmeshed in her day-to-day existence, but on the other hand, her sadness had become the defining feature of her connection to Chris. Sheena assured me she was open to letting the sadness go.

As she spoke about Chris, Sheena's Scottish accent seemed to intensify. "Chris always knew that I was never, ever ashamed of him. Never! Not once. He knew I would speak openly about these issues and how much I loved him, but I was never ashamed."

Chris had died as the result of a drug overdose.

"I think it was accidental," she told me. "I've got no evidence to say that it wasn't. But so many times Chris told me that he'd had enough."

Once again, I found myself being drawn in to the emotion of the story. So often it felt like I entered into a bubble containing the world of my client. I said a silent prayer that I'd be able to help her. Sheena continued: "People are very sympathetic and empathic at the beginning, but they get fed up listening to you. So, I'm always very aware of other people... not boring them with my grief. Do you know what I mean?" she asked.

I'd heard this so many times before from my clients. Their fear of burdening others with their grief, the sense that the world moved on around them while their devastation and sadness remained. They often felt helpless to regain their sense of self. Their world had irrevocably changed and caught up in a swirling and unpredictable tide of grief, they struggled to find purchase to right themselves, to find a new sense of direction.

"Maybe it's also to do with what I don't want other people to see. I don't know really, to be honest, Tom."

I prepared Sheena for the session by going through the usual instructions for the IADC protocol. Rather than using the eye movement software, she felt better suited to the self-tapping of the 'butterfly hug' method. But before we processed her sadness, I needed her to fully access it. By getting her talking about Chris, she'd activate crucial memories. The memory networks of the brain are where the emotions associated with a traumatic loss are stored.

"Tell me about his personality," I asked. This was one of several specific questions I knew would help activate the part of her brain we needed to access.

"He was a very warm person. He had a huge, big heart and he loved people. And people loved him. He was funny. He had a good sense of humour, and he liked a good laugh. But he was so caught up in all the mess that he was embroiled in that his personality was hidden. I'm very aware that the person he was showing himself as, and the person other people were seeing, wasn't the real Chris. And that was because of the drugs and all the stuff that he was involved in, all the traumas that he put himself through, and all the scary situations that he ended up in. There's so many different faces of Chris that I've seen, and I've seen them in so many different situations that it's difficult…" she trailed off.

Sheena had told me about the good aspects of Chris's personality, and she'd hinted at some dark times, but I wondered whether Sheena was reluctant to tell me about the aspects of Chris that drew him into a life of drug abuse and even crime. Was she afraid to look behind the walls she kept up for years to protect herself from the intensity of her own emotions? I needed her to go there if she was going to fully access her sadness, and therefore fully benefit from the therapy.

"Tell me a bit about some of these shadow sides. What were the worst faces of Chris? What were the parts of his personality that ended up with him in prison, or using drugs?" I asked.

In a way, I was provoking Sheena's emotions. If clients hold back on the full intensity of their story, it also hinders how well the processing will work. As Dr Botkin would say: never underestimate a client's determination to avoid the intensity of their own emotions. Hopefully, Sheena would break through those walls. I needed her to really *feel* it.

"He wanted to fit in," she continued, "he wanted to be one of the boys. But Chris always had to be the best at it. Instead of sticking with the things he was good at, he would end up becoming involved in the murky side of stuff," she told me.

"It was like he was trying to be good at the things that were not good for him?", I asked.

"Yes, absolutely. I used to always think, 'Why can't you try to be good at the things that are good for you?' But he didn't fit in. He wasn't hugely academic at school. But he was very good looking, he was very charming, and the girls loved him. Yet he would end up in these horrendous situations. Getting bashed and ending up in hospital. And I would think, 'Maybe this time things will work out', and it just never would. It was always a bloody shambles, and I would get called in cause obviously, I was his mother, his saviour. Do you know what I mean? Of course I was his saviour. No one else."

I asked Sheena when it all started.

"Oh, gosh, right from the beginning! He was using Valium and things, and he was only twelve! His Dad had just left, and he had decided he wanted to kill himself. One day he tried to throw himself in front of a bus, and I was lying on top of him, trying to keep him safe. And I tried to get help for him. But because he was only twelve people didn't take his problems seriously, they thought I was just a mother who couldn't cope, which was just ridiculous."

These were painful memories. I could see Sheena's tears reflected in the light of her computer screen. She was really accessing her sadness now. It was tough, but this would help her later. We needed to identify specific pieces of sadness as targets for processing with bilateral stimulation.

"There was always this huge fear of something happening to him. Of him not having food or being cold. And then he would phone me. He would phone in the middle of the night and say 'Mum, I'm stuck in Glasgow, and there's people chasing me with knives.' I would be saying to him, 'Where are you?' And he said, 'I don't know where I am', and I'd be running about Glasgow trying to find him. And I had no help. It was always me, on my own, trying to find him and fix him and help him. It was unbearable. And then there was just constant things with drugs and people coming to the door looking for money. I was living this respectable life as a nurse, looking after people who had drug and alcohol problems – that was my job. And I was living this life of absolute horror at home, trying to keep my son alive and safe. I was just always terrified… that he was going to be killed. That was my big terror, my big horror, and my big fear."

Then one day, her big fear came true. Away on holiday with her new partner, Sheena got a phone call. Chris had overdosed on heroin and died.

When I asked Sheena what part of the story of Chris' life and death brought up the most sadness for her, she said "Why could he not have had that chance – like some of his friends who have been through issues and problems, and they've managed to go on with their lives and they're happy – why could he not have just been a rebellious teenager and then come out of it?"

Sheena commenced the bilateral stimulation by alternately tapping her shoulders with arms crossed over her chest. "It just feels really dark inside me," she said after the first set.

"Well, you're doing a really good job, Sheena," I reassured her. "I just want you to let yourself go into those feelings. Step into it. Don't try to manage it in any way. Just let yourself feel it, and whenever you're ready, when you're feeling it, you can start tapping again."

Tears rolled quietly down her face as she tapped away. After the next set was done, I asked Sheena what she noticed about her sadness – was it changing?

"I found myself feeling as if I was trying to see Chris… as if I was trying to look for him," she said.

"What did you notice over that set – about your sadness?" I asked. I didn't want Sheena 'looking' for Chris. At this stage of the processing, that was likely to slow our progress. Sheena replied that she was allowing herself to feel her sadness, that she was allowing thoughts and memories to arise, and that this was bringing on more tears. Thoughts and memories that naturally and spontaneously arise are fine, but I didn't want her directing the experience. Her focus needed to be primarily on the emotions she's feeling, not getting caught up in thoughts.

The task of IADC therapy is a delicate one. It is aggressive in that it directs clients – sometimes relentlessly – into recalling the most painful experience of their lives. But we also need to hold them in that space with gentle support; to recognise the inherent fragility that comes with such overwhelming sadness over the loss of their loved one. My deep respect for the courage Sheena was showing made me remind myself to stay focused, to not miss this moment; my opportunity to hopefully help her in a profound way. That meant encouraging her as we went, while also insisting she follow my directions to ensure the therapy would be effective.

"I want you to let yourself feel your feelings, which you're doing a really good job of Sheena. You're doing great. And that's gonna be our starting point. The starting point is feeling those emotions. And as you start tapping, you're just going to go with whatever happens. So, if memories or thoughts arise, that's fine, but we don't want to direct them. We don't want to look for memories, and we don't want to try to make anything happen in terms of seeing Chris. There's going to be plenty of time for that. And if that happens, you're just going to let it come to you. It's going to happen *to* you. It's not going to be something that you cause to happen, okay? So don't feel like you need to go looking for him. He's going to come to you when the time is right.

"Be more like an observer. As long as you're feeling those emotions in the beginning, and you do the tapping, then you're just going along for the ride. You're going to see what happens. So just allow yourself to feel that sadness wherever it is at right now. The sadness that Chris' life couldn't have turned out better and differently. And whenever you're feeling that you can start tapping."

Following the next set, we made fast and steady progress. Sheena's tears continued to fall, but she reported that she was feeling calmer. Feeling somehow supported. She soon began to spontaneously recall happy memories of Chris, from when he was younger. Then she had one of those spontaneous realisations I had come to see as normal in IADC therapy – comforting insights that seem to come out of nowhere.

"I just thought of something Chris told me a long time ago. When he realised how seriously concerned and worried I was – constantly – and how it was all impacting me, he said to me 'Mum, a lot of the time you think that my life's just absolute misery. But half of that time I'm actually having a ball.'"

We continued to make progress. Peeling back layers of grief – not just from Chris' death but also the dozens of traumas leading up to it. Sheena expressed that she was feeling some guilt. Was she responsible for the way her son's life had turned out? By marrying a man who was "a pig", had she contributed to the murky path he'd ended up on, filled with drugs and violence and crime? We did a set on that, which resulted in a greater feeling of "balance", and by the end of Day 1, Sheena had processed a lot of sadness, she felt calmer, and was noticing happy memories and feelings. She also felt a sense of gratitude and appreciation for Chris' life.

"I've got a feeling of just… peacefulness. And I'm wondering if that's kind of how *he* feels."

When I logged on to our Zoom call the next evening, I was eager to maintain the momentum from the day before. But before I could charge into the bilateral stimulation, I needed to check on how she was feeling, if any other pieces of sadness had arisen, or if she had experienced some kind of after-death communication which would occasionally occur in-between sessions.

As it turns out, she had.

"We had a team-building day today, with work. It was fun. But it was also strange. I was telling the girls when we were getting in the car about what I'd done last night. I said, 'I wonder if I'll get any sign or something from Chris? My friend Petra says, 'Just wait and see'. So we're driving up to the place, and I said to my boss, 'So what is it that we're doing?' She says, 'We're going to be painting'. It would be a painting class, and we'd all have a go at doing our own version of the same painting. Then she said, 'Oh, it's sunflowers.'

"Petra and I both know the connection that Chris and I have around sunflowers. I've got a sunflower tattoo on my leg. I'm also wearing a sunflower necklace. Chris's casket was covered in sunflowers – and only sunflowers – when he passed away. That was our flower. And it was Chris'."

"Wow," I said.

"I know it's weird. My painting was actually really good! I'm not good at painting, ever. But it's really good, and I'm dead proud of it, you know? And I was talking to one of the other girls, and she says 'That's funny, because it's Mother's Day on Sunday. So maybe that's Chris's gift to you… this sunflower picture.' It made me feel really happy. It made me feel really connected with him," she said.

For Sheena, the specific subject of the painting day – sunflowers – was symbolic of Chris. Her tattoo, her necklace, the flowers on his casket, they were all strongly representative of Chris and his life and death. The proximity to Mothers' Day, and my sessions with her, made this symbol especially poignant. It wasn't for me to say if the sunflower painting was a sign from Chris. But it was precisely the kind of thing Bill and Judy Guggenheim's research in *Hello from Heaven* found was a source of comfort and meaning for many grieving people, a finding that more recent ADC research has also confirmed.

My focus quickly returned to the task at hand. I wanted us to go deeper today… into and through the remaining pieces of sadness, and deeper into the feelings of peace, love and gratitude that were starting to permeate Sheena's consciousness the night before. Even better than a symbolic ADC would be helping facilitate a direct perception of Chris' presence.

We moved into the processing again. Tears flowed as we worked through her memories of many traumatic incidents, including the harrowing moment she had to identify Chris' body in the mortuary after racing home from her holiday in Spain. She had imagined that he'd be lying in some kind of hospital bed, but when the curtains opened for Sheena to view her son's body, he was just lying there on a slab. Sheena screamed until the kind lady who'd pulled back the curtains broke protocol and let her in the room. He'd just had his hair done the day before he died. He looked just like he was sleeping. But when she touched him, he was cold. This was the moment it all became real for Sheena.

After another set of tapping Sheena reported feeling some strange sensations.

"It was as if I was being sucked out of my body," she said with a curious tone. "Very, very weird that. There's just kind of an atmosphere in the room."

I continued with the IADC protocol. After the next set, she said: "Such a strong feeling! I don't know if I was falling asleep a wee bit or something. I don't know... it was the strangest feeling as if I was getting pulled out of my body. And there was all this strange noise going on, and there was a real strange atmosphere. There's still a strange atmosphere in the room."

"Does it feel like it relates to Chris?" I asked.

"Yes, definitely! I don't know if it was his voice, but something came into my head and it was saying: 'Why are you wearing that stupid ring?'"

Sheena was wearing a new ring. She felt something touching her finger, and then her knee. She wondered if this was her imagination, her mind playing tricks on her. Following the next set, she spoke slowly after she opened her eyes. "I just had this feeling of Chris and I having this conversation. And he said, 'I'm okay, Mum.'"

Sheena sat quietly as the emotion washed over her. She leant back in her chair and closed her eyes again, breathing rhythmically. I assumed she was still feeling his presence. Another silent tear ran down her cheek. Sheena's ADC had commenced, and now I needed to keep her relaxed to allow her to go deeper into the experience. This is where the most impactful healing could occur.

I initiated another set of tapping. "Just allow yourself to feel that connection to Chris, and don't judge it at all. Just let it unfold. Let it happen. You're doing really well. Just let yourself stay very relaxed. Just be open to whatever happens."

She felt more touches, but I could tell she was also getting tired. The sessions had gone well, but I wanted to see if we could get the absolute maximum out of them. She'd come this far…

"Is there anything you would want to say to Chris, or ask him?" I asked.

Sheena's voice was soft and slow now, but it wavered with emotion. "I'd like to know if he's at peace. But I know he is." She pondered it further. "I'd like to know if he's with other people. Does he feel loved? That's something that's really important, that he's not alone." I had to push back my own emotions; I squinted as I held back my own tears.

At the end of this set, Sheena was quiet with her eyes closed for several minutes. She was immersed in an ADC. When she eventually opened her eyes, she explained "I was picturing in my head all the people who have gone before. I was picturing my dad, my mum. But my mum was young!" Sheena seemed genuinely surprised at what she was reporting. This, too, is a common feature of ADCs – they are usually not what the client is expecting. "These are people who passed over. Chris's friend Stephen – who was like his partner in crime – he passed away as well.

"And I had a picture in my head of Chris and Steven, like lying on a this like grassy bank smoking a ciggie. And Cindy, the dog – I saw her as well! Chris was lying there, smoking his ciggie, as if to say to me, 'Look, Mum.' (she moved her arm in a sweeping motion). 'There are all these people here!'"

Sheena was smiling now, with a look of amazement. She was crying again, but these weren't tears of sadness.

"So did that answer your question?' I asked. I couldn't hide my smile.

She nodded through the tears. In a moment she caught her breath and continued. "Aunty Susie was there as well – who Chris loved. And Chris' dad's dad was there. He looked happy, actually. They all looked as if they were happy together. But Chris and Stephen were on this grassy bank... up to mischief I think, for the looks of 'em! He went like this 'Look, Mum [waves her arm]. Of course I'm happy.'

"Wow," she said. "It's very strange, isn't it? But he looked totally relaxed. Chilled out, and just, like... 'Look, Mum.'" She made the arm movement again. "It's quite lovely, isn't it?" she said.

Sheena's courage had been rewarded. Her rapid-fire visual ADC included many people who had passed but who she was not focused on at all and didn't anticipate connecting with, including Aunty Susie, their pet dog, and Sheena's ex-husband's father. And just as I had been surprised when Nanna appeared younger in my ADC, Sheena's mum was younger as well. Despite the unexpected nature of her ADC, it perfectly answered her question. Chris wasn't alone. He came across to her as just fine – happy even – and as cheeky as ever.

It had been an intense couple of evenings. My brain felt like sludge from all the concentration and emotion; I could only imagine what it was like for Sheena. But the outcome was more than worth it. If the sunflower painting was a very cool Mother's Day gift, Sheena's experience tonight was even better. I asked her how she felt now.

"Totally exhausted," she shook her head. "But very peaceful. A bit emotional.... And a bit annoyed... he doesn't like my ring!" she laughed. "Cheeky boy! That's the kind of thing he would've said."

When I contacted Sheena a couple of weeks later to check in on her, she replied:

Hi Tom
I've been having lots of dreams with Chris in them.
I've been feeling a real closeness to him.
I've been great, thanks.
Sheena

Chapter 11

Darkness Descends

One of the many blessings in my life is the little holiday home by the beach that Mum's parents, Nanny and Grandpa, bought in the late 1970's. Just eighty metres back from the clifftop at Port Willunga on South Australia's mid-coast, the yellow brick house provided the backdrop of so many childhood memories: summer holidays spent swimming, body boarding, and playing spotlight in the backyard with my brothers and school friends until bedtime.

This particular Easter long weekend was a far cry from those childhood holidays. As I drove along the final two kilometres to the beach house – with my miniature schnauzer Rupert in the seat beside me and bags and stuff piled in the back – I pondered the grey clouds above. Despite the seasonal warmth there was a humid, stormy feel in the air.

In just minutes, I'd be meeting Annabel and Jasper, having finished up with my last client for the day about an hour before. We had close friends coming down to stay with us, and a holiday Monday to boot. I should have been excited but instead, I was apprehensive. Even more than that... I felt a knot in the pit of my stomach.

At sixteen months of age, Jasper was the apple of our eye, but all-consuming, as toddlers are. Annabel especially was burdened with a chronic lack of sleep. My professional self understood and was sympathetic to her irritability and low mood. I was doing everything I could to help her keep postnatal depression at bay. But as a husband I was deeply concerned for her, and our relationship. My heart was filled with gratitude and awe at her motherly instincts. But I struggled to separate myself from the personal hurt of the aloofness and bickering that had appeared between us.

Did you know the highest rate of divorce is in couples with children aged zero to five? Well, that doesn't surprise me one bit. I was stressed and worried. Annabel and Jasper were the most important things in my life, but life had been feeling hard lately. Would we be able to pull ourselves out of this cycle of stress and resentment, or was it going to get worse and spiral out of control? I recognised my catastrophic thoughts for what they were. This would all pass. How I feel now is not a prediction of the future. A weekend away is probably just what we need, I thought.

As I turned the corner onto the road that led from the expressway to the beach, I reached over, stroked Rupert's black coat, and glanced up at the gathering clouds. Normally a master of helpful self-talk I would've thought my mood would lighten accordingly, but it didn't. I just couldn't shake the feeling that something was wrong. The feeling of dread lingered.

Over the weekend Jasper developed a temperature. He had no other symptoms of anything being wrong. We gave him Dymadon which could keep it at bay temporarily, but it kept coming back. And by the Sunday night we were starting to get concerned. Jess, a friend who was staying with us, was on the phone to her mother, Margie, an emergency room nurse. Margie gently urged: if you're concerned, take him to the emergency department, just to be sure. So, at about six o'clock that night Annabel, Jasper and I went to the hospital to get him checked out.

Endless minutes waiting turned into hours as the doctors and nurses took blood samples and checked Jasper over. To take the blood they used the tedious finger prick method, meaning you have to hold your distressed child as the nurse tries to collect enough drops of blood from the pricked finger to run a blood test. After what seemed like forever, a young doctor with a concerned look came and found us in the waiting area.

"I'm afraid we need to take the blood again. There's something wrong with our machine. We're so sorry. We'll do the second test on a different machine and try to get the results as quickly as we can."

At close to midnight he returned and sat down next to us, speaking carefully and quietly. There was nothing wrong with the machine. Jasper's blood results were so abnormal they assumed the machine was broken. Something *was* wrong.

"Well, what's causing this?", I asked.

It could be diet, he said. There could be a number of causes. But if it was severe enough to show such extreme results it didn't make any sense to me that it was his diet. Jasper ate normal healthy food.

The next day Dr Lawrence came in. A straightforward lady with glasses, she emanated an air of capability such that I assumed she was very senior in her role. She pressed on Jasper's abdomen as part of her examination. She was deliberate, turning her head as she felt for something in his tummy, almost like she was trying to hear what someone was whispering nearby. "It's probably constipation," she said, but we'd need an X-Ray to find out why she could feel a lump.

A couple of hours later, a nurse hurriedly entered the hospital room. It wasn't constipation, she said. The referral letter even speculated on the diagnosis, but we didn't know what the medical jargon meant.

The nurse's body language and sense of urgency told us it wasn't good.

"We've called ahead to the Women's and Children's Hospital. They're expecting you. You should get him down there pronto," the nurse urged.

Our heads were spinning. Adrenaline kicked in, and we did as we were told. I wanted to get Jasper to the doctors who could help him as soon as humanly possible. We drove straight there.

The Emergency Department on this Easter long weekend was bursting at the seams, a whirling hive of activity. I paced the cubicle as Jasper slept, nearing midnight, when a nurse, then a doctor, then another nurse came in. I was alert, trying to follow what was happening, to get any clue of what was wrong with my baby boy. Did we have any family history of tumours? they asked.

Jasper was admitted, and the next day we had an initial meeting with a surgical registrar, a very friendly pregnant lady in blue scrubs. The conference room had a whiteboard and desks pushed together to create a sort of table. They needed to do more tests, she said, but they were pretty sure the tentative diagnosis was correct. How did we go from constipation to a tumour? We were devastated. A million questions raced through my head, but I could only compute so much news at once.

"We always aim for a cure," she said with a compassionate look that did very little to reassure me.

Annabel and I sat there, holding each other, dumbfounded and heartbroken.

The days that followed were a blur of tests, meetings, and more tests. All the while our little boy cuddled us and cooed, trying his first words, and walking in his toddler like way when he had the chance to play with toys on the ward. Whenever he could, he would waddle to the play area, with a canula bandaged to his arm. His favourite toy was the kitchen set. He wore a white chef's hat, a little striped t-shirt, and a nappy, cooking imaginary dishes and giggling as I devoured them: "Nom nom nom nom nom." I smiled at Jasper as we played, but inside, a sense of desperation overwhelmed me. There has to be an answer! There has to be a way to fix this!

I remained alert, the protective Dad. I wanted to know what was going on at all times and quizzed the doctors politely but assertively. I sent the food tray back immediately when the orderly delivered Jasper a meal right as he was meant to be fasting before a procedure. Then they came to draw blood from him when he was just a couple of hours away from a general anaesthetic. Why not take it from him when he's under, and prod him one less time while he's awake? The nurse agreed and left.

I thought I was going to end up hating the hospital, but I didn't. Although the staff weren't perfect, they genuinely cared. This was the place where he could get the care he needs. Part of me wanted to study and learn everything I could to ensure nothing was missed, but I stopped myself. I didn't want to become an expert on childhood cancer. There's no way in a short space of time I could compete with the knowledge of the experienced oncologists. As a psychologist, I wasn't medically trained, but I could follow along with their clinical way of thinking and some of the jargon. No, I decided, I'd be more effective holding the doctors and nurses accountable by asking questions. What's the prognosis? What are the risks of this procedure or that test? Why are we doing this? Is this an evidence-based protocol? Are there any options you haven't considered?

Annabel and I cried and cried. We supported each other as best we could, in between being strong in front of Jasper and trying to follow along with whirlwind of conversations and procedures involved in trying to confirm the diagnosis.

Fluorescent lights seemed to distort my sense of time. The hospital smell became so familiar as to seem normal. The knot in my stomach was now a permanent resident.

More than anything I'd ever wanted in my life, I wanted Jasper to be okay. In between crying, praying, and questioning the nursing and medical staff, I tried to do everything I could to help him be okay. I recognised that the only meaning he would give to the predicament he was in, was through his perspective as a sixteen-month-old toddler. He didn't have the sense of desperation and despair we did. I wanted him to be as comfortable and happy as he possibly could. I tried to think of every which way I could protect him from the nightmare that was unfolding.

I recalled the movie *Life is Beautiful,* in which the lead character played by Roberto Begnini lovingly tries to shield his son from the reality of a prisoner of war camp in which they find themselves captive. He convinces his son it's all a game. The guards are in on it too, so they'd need to hide very well and follow the rules in order to win a grand prize at the end.

As we rolled his hospital bed down the corridors to the operating room I'd make racing car sounds, with screeching tyre noises when we rounded a corner. I bought a surgical mask from the pharmacy and we played with it endlessly, putting it on and off his teddy bears, and each other, as a form of exposure to make it less distressing when he had to go into theatre. I bought him a little toy van from the hospital cafeteria, with wind-up wheels that would scoot across the floor. And a little toy puppy dog that we named 'Little Rupert'.

I wanted to protect Annabel, too. Only one parent could stay overnight, and there was no way she was going to be separated from Jasper. Annabel's mum owned an Air B'n'B property near the hospital, so I stayed there. Annabel was so attuned to his needs 24/7, I could tell she was exhausted, but she never complained.

I tried to shield Annabel from distressing things when I could. In the anteroom of an imaging suite, I had to help a nurse hold Jasper down – screaming – as he was forced to drink a foul-tasting medicine before yet another procedure. I didn't blame him, I could smell it. Couldn't those know-it-all scientists make this shit at least taste like something better than radioactive waste?! We forced him to drink it. The only reason I complied is because the test would help figure out what the tumour was, it was crucial to him getting the right treatment. We needed that test!

I took him into the surgical theatre, distracting him as the anaesthetist placed the mask over his face and his little nappy-clad body went limp. Standing next to the exit door, a kind older lady placed her hand on my arm, silently giving me permission to take a minute to compose myself before the electric door would open and I'd have to greet Annabel and reassure her that everything went fine. Taking deep breaths and wiping tears away with my handkerchief, I wondered whether that was the lady's actual job.

One morning, after being in the hospital for four days, Jasper toddled over to his shoes and tried to put them on. He didn't have the words to say it, but I knew. He was telling us he wanted to go home.

That night, just like the nights before, once Annabel and Jasper had turned out the light in their hospital room, I made the five-minute walk up the street to the Air B'n'B.

I contemplated the worst.

I cried and I prayed. *Please, God, don't take my little boy!*

I pleaded for the help of my grandparents. If they were there in the afterlife, in the realm of spirit, couldn't they do something?

If Nanna could visit me the night before the Sydney Cup and tell me we were going to win, couldn't I reach her somehow and ask her to intervene to save the life of the great-grandson she never met? I called out in my mind. *Nanna, please help!* I didn't hear anything back.

An ocean of desperation was now my home. I cried more. I prayed more. I tried to keep my business running as best I could, with the incredible kindness and help of my business partner Nick.

I was struggling through each day driven by my love for my beautiful son, and the fear that his life was now in danger. Was *my* life destined to be defined by grief? How on Earth would we get through this? Eventually, sheer exhaustion would rein my thoughts in, bring me back to the present. I still had to be up early to get back to the hospital, to get through the next day.

Deep in the inky darkness of that Air B'n'B's unfamiliar bedroom, I had never felt so alone. All I could muster was a final prayer for my son, before exhaustion took over, luring me into a fitful sleep.

In dark days, small kindnesses take on a new meaning. When a nurse would bring extra apple juice and biscuits. Or a friend from Annabel's mum's group made home-cooked food for Jasper. Or a doctor who took extra time to make sure we fully understood the next test or procedure, and patiently answered our questions.

Fin Klein, the pastor from one of the schools where we were running my Healthy Minds program, heard the news about Jasper and called. He was calm and caring, but somehow matter of fact in the way he spoke. He'd clearly supported people through situations like this before. I walked through the park next to the hospital as we spoke on the phone, and tears silently rolled down my face as Finn asked me if I would like him to say a prayer for Jasper. For a non-religious bloke, I was sure doing a hell of a lot of praying.

The revolving door of doctors and nurses continued. We think we know what it is, they said. Just a couple more tests to be sure. We need to confirm the diagnosis in order to give him the best treatment. But I could read the room: this wasn't good.

Through it all Annabel never stopped loving Jasper, and me, with all her heart. The niggles and the arguments had instantly faded into the background. Our little family mattered more than anything in the world to us, and we would do anything – absolutely anything – to keep it going and return to our usual life.

One night before they switched out the light in their hospital room and I'd start my walk up the hill, Jasper looked right at me with his blue eyes, smiling. He stretched out his little arms for a cuddle.

"Daddy!" he said, beaming.

I picked Jasper up and held him close to me as he snuggled his face into my neck.

I never wanted to let go.

Chapter 12

Bianca

Bianca and Jochen had the kind of relationship everyone dreams of. Their love seemed to grow, not diminish, with time.

"My relationship with him was perfect," she told me over our Zoom call. "He really loved me. I felt like I was his queen – he treated me like a queen for 23 years. He put me up on a pedestal…" She started to cry. "And I think that's the one thing that really I'm struggling with, because there's no one who will love me as much anymore."

They were so in touch with each other, they knew immediately if something was wrong with the other. If Jochen had had a bad day, Bianca would know in an instant. If something was bothering her, he would know, and immediately ask how he could help. "He would take one look at my face and know if I was upset or if something was bothering me… because we were so in tune. That's what it felt like. It was a soul connection."

Despite his emotional attunement to Bianca, Jochen was a strong personality who could be direct to the point of being brutal. "He didn't have much of a filter," she told me. "And he had a strong presence. You knew when he was in the room."

The day Jochen died, he was helping a friend. "He was always out there helping mates, helping everyone, helping my family. He would stop in the middle of a road to help people. That's his personality."

It was hot work in the summer sun, helping his friend fix a concreting truck. With Jochen's engineering background, and as a problem-solver by nature, he was often the one people would go to when something needed to be fixed. When he came inside for a drink, Bianca had no idea it would be their last conversation. Jochen was dieting, and she'd made him a broccoli bake for dinner.

"I was ironing, and he said, 'I don't think I'll ever have dinner. That's it for me.'"

She thought Jochen's wording was odd.

"I said: 'for the rest of your life?' And he just like looked at me as he was having a drink, and he said, 'No. No more for me.'"

Later in the afternoon Jochen fell from the concrete truck he was working on, hitting his head. He lost consciousness for a while but then stood up. By the time Bianca got to Jochen, he was seated but she knew how serious it was because of the pool of blood where he'd landed. She held his hand, desperate to know her soulmate would be okay. Jochen didn't say anything; he just closed his eyes.

"I knew he didn't want me to see him like that. He was in so much pain, and he didn't want me to see him in so much pain."

At the hospital, doctors had talked about having two choices: to operate, or not. But with a severe brain injury, there were no guarantees he would survive, and if he did, he might never be the same. Jochen's big personality might be lost forever, confined to an existence of limited functioning with continual dependence on others. "He might not even recognize you," Bianca recounted what the doctors told her. "Or he might not be able to walk anymore – or things like that."

It was at this point Bianca was confronted with her greatest fear – that Jochen might die – because the doctors wanted to know how much to intervene in the event he was at risk of severe neurological disability. Did he plan anything? Had they discussed his wishes?

"I started crying because that previous night was Saturday night, and he had to talk to his brother in Germany. His mum was quite sick, and they thought she was getting dementia. She was refusing treatment and getting really aggressive to the nurses. Jochen was crying – he had tears in his eyes – and said: 'Promise me, if the brain goes, I go!'"

The doctors saw the shock on her face as she relayed the conversation from the night before. But despite what he'd said, Bianca wasn't ready to let Jochen go. "I said, 'I've got power of attorney. I'm his wife, and I decide. Do whatever it takes – whatever it costs. I just want him back. I just want to bring him home.'"

The doctors excused themselves to deliberate on the situation, before returning.

"Jochen has decided for you," they told her. His pupils were already fixed and dilated. They were not going to operate.

I explained the IADC therapy protocol to Bianca and asked her what her strongest piece of sadness was. This would provide our starting point.

"The strongest bit of sadness…" Bianca's speech was staccato as she drew breaths in between sobs. I was having to rein in my emotions now, too. I hoped Bianca wouldn't notice. She didn't need to be distracted by a red-eyed grief therapist with a frog in his throat, she needed a professional. Thankfully, as I took a sip from the water bottle next to my computer, she was absorbed by her loving memories of Jochen, and her deep sadness from missing him: "I remember that every single night and every single morning… we would hug, really, really close to each other. We would trace each other's faces, and I will never get that anymore. I used to trace his eyes, when he had his eyes closed. He used to do the same to me, he would trace my lips. We would just stare into each other's eyes."

I had her follow the blue ball I had on her screen using my bilateral stimulation software. She was immediately able to step into her sadness. The preparatory questions I had asked of her had already started this process, but the bilateral stimulation of the eye movements helped her enter the 'core' of her grief: the deep sadness of the loss of her beloved Jochen. On the downside, she was having trouble tracking the blue bull moving horizontally across her screen because she was crying intensely. I had to encourage her in a gentle but assertive way: "Keep going, Bianca, you're doing great."

I needed her to keep her eyes tracking in order for the processing to work. In traditional EMDR, the practitioner would often take their client to a 'safe place' when experiencing extreme distress, but we don't do that in IADC. For the sake of grief therapy, it is a mistake to abort the process when the client is experiencing their strongest emotions, as this is when the therapy is doing its most important job: reducing the intense sadness associated with the thoughts and memories of the person who died. We don't want to only process moderate sadness, we want to process all of it, especially the most distressing parts.

I urged Bianca on, and courageously she continued to track the ball. After only the third set, she reported: "He's telling me: 'Don't be sad, I am still hugging you.'"

Bianca was overwhelmed with emotion now, and I wasn't sure I heard her correctly. I turned up the volume on my computer.

"Sorry, Bianca, can you just say that again?" I gently urged, keen to hear what was happening for her in that moment.

"In my brain, he was telling me, I heard his voice. 'Don't be sad, I am still hugging you. I am just here.'" Bianca was feeling Jochen's presence and hearing his words. Her ADC had begun.

She had slipped so easily into her connection with Jochen, and she was so emotional, that I wanted her to be able to immerse herself in it, without needing to track the ball with her eyes. I needed to shift gear and let it naturally unfold.

"Okay, Bianca, what I'm going to get you to do, just to let you be in that moment... We're just going to try a little bit of tapping where you can keep your eyes closed for a while, okay? So if you're feeling Jochen, and hearing him... just use your arms." I demonstrated the butterfly hug technique and explained the next part of the process.

It was quite amazing, on one hand, that she was already in the throes of a connection with her late husband. But I had learned to not be fazed by anything in IADC therapy anymore. It really was that powerful.

She started tapping. "Just go with whatever happens," I assured her. She leant back in her chair, tapping her shoulders with arms crossed over her chest. She seemed calm all of a sudden. The distress of a few moments ago was gone.

"Just let me know what you were noticing then," I asked.

"He's just holding me..." she said dreamily, sniffling, and closed her eyes again as if slipping back into the sensation of being held by Jochen.

"He's calming me.... He's placing his hands on my shoulders. It is calming."

After the next set, Bianca started to doubt her experience. "I feel more calm feelings," she said. "But there's a thought in my head that says it's my brain playing tricks on me. Was he really here?" She paused, as if listening. "He's asking me: 'Have I ever let you down?' And I said 'no'. He said, 'I will never let you down.' He's just here, so it's quite calming. As crazy as it sounds... he's just sitting here. His arms are on my shoulders."

Bianca opened her eyes. Her attention was back with me. "I don't know how this is in my brain, but I'm turning 50 in a few weeks, and I was really upset because he's not with me. But then, he said, 'I'll be with you for that.' It's really stupid, but it's more like he's saying: whatever I plan to do, he's with me anyway. So why worry about it?"

As we did more sets of tapping, she felt her sadness further reducing, and eventually, good feelings started to come in. She started to look relaxed. Happy even.

"I'm smiling because this conversation is happening at the moment. He's sitting right here. It's going to be fine."

We were making such rapid progress I couldn't imagine how a client could confect this response. Even the most floridly wishful thinker couldn't manufacture the emotional changes I was witnessing. She was feeling her loved one right there with her. On a subsequent set of tapping, she became emotional again, but explained, "He kissed me on the side of the head, that's what brought up the tears. But it was calming."

We finished the first session with her feeling very calm. We'd made miles of progress. Her demeanour was serene. She felt Jochen with her. He would never let her down, and she knew she would be fine. "That's the conversation I've wanted to get these last 13 months since Jochen died," Bianca told me with a look of relief and satisfaction on her face. She was feeling peaceful for the first time since his death.

I was in awe of Bianca's courage. She didn't know me at all apart from the brief screening call we'd had about six weeks earlier to determine her eligibility for my research study. Yet here she was, willingly stepping in to the worst parts of the worst thing that had ever happened in her life. This was the paradox of IADC therapy: by stepping into it, she'd be able to get to the other side of it.

On the second day, Bianca reported that she'd had a nap after our session, then went out for some groceries. And as she was waiting at the lights, she felt overwhelmed with gratitude for her marriage.

"When I was driving home, I had this overwhelming feeling of being so lucky. I was so lucky to have had 23 years of that," she said. "That never crossed my mind in the last 13 months, but driving along I was actually watching the traffic wondering how many of these people had never experienced what we had."

Bianca had made significant progress on moving through her grief, but I wanted to make even more. And I knew there was close to a 100% chance that she would have an ADC again today, given how easily she felt Jochen's presence the day before. We started by assessing the strongest piece of sadness in the moment: it was the idea of facing life alone without him. It didn't take long. After a few sets of eye movements, she reported feeling Jochen's presence again.

"I felt his arms around me… so that's already unfolding," she said, almost matter-of-factly.

"You told me earlier there was something you wanted to say to him. Can you tell me what that was?" I asked.

"He would always say he was a lucky man, and I would go along with it." She flashed a cheeky smile. "But I want to tell him how lucky *I* was."

"Well, let's do that now. Keep that in mind and follow the blue ball," I said as I administered the eye movements and had Bianca close her eyes as usual. She sat silently with her eyes closed for several minutes.

"I told him how lucky I was that he chose me; that I was the one he poured his love into over the last 23 years. He just cupped my face, looking at me while I was talking to him. And he said, 'You know I really love you.' I said 'yes'. He just hugged me, and it was really comforting. He said: 'Rest in that love'. I always wanted to feel his hug one more time."

I wanted to help Bianca formulate any questions or unresolved issues she wanted to address. ADCs are usually not fragile. She was in a receptive state, was feeling his presence strongly, so I knew she'd be able to go back into the experience. Bianca told me she wanted to know if Jochen was okay. "I hope he's not suffering. I always used to know everything that was going on with him."

"Let's ask him," I replied.

After another set of tapping, her ADC continued.

"I was actually looking at the side of his head, where the injury was. He said everything was okay. And he was showing me his knees. He has always had problems with his knees, and said 'it's no problem now'. His knees are fine. And I got this message of... now he's a part of me. I don't need to worry about it anymore because I carry him with me. I feel so much love!"

Bianca was beaming. Her tear-soaked face shone. During the final set of bilateral stimulation Bianca asked Jochen, "What do I do now?

"He said 'keep doing what you're doing'. Continue to look after Julian (our son), get the tree cut... all these practical things that are happening in everyday life. You're doing well at work, keep doing that. And don't worry too much about the future.'"

Bianca was crying again now, but her body language communicated relief. "They're actually happy tears," she told me. "These are not sad tears. It's reassuring that... it'll be fine."

Bianca and I both knew that she would still have tough days ahead of her. But now she had a newfound strength. She had an ongoing bond with Jochen that was comforting, reassuring, and strong.

As I reflected on my sessions with Bianca, it occurred to me that this was a powerful manifestation of the 'continuing bonds' theory of grief. The leading experts in grief research – like Professor Robert Neimeyer, and others – recognise the benefits of maintaining a sense of the continuing presence of a deceased loved one. Unlike decades gone by, where the grieving person was encouraged to accept the finality of the loss in order to move forward, the continuing bonds theory says it can be both normal and beneficial to maintain the relationship in some way.

I followed up with Bianca a few weeks later. She replied:

Hi Tom,

I've been okay, feeling more at peace.

Although I have been emotional last night as it's my birthday today and Jochen should have been here to celebrate with me.

Thanks for checking in.

P.S. I have been dreaming of him more often, like almost every night, since the sessions. I feel him near - not sure if it's my brain playing tricks, but I like it. It gives me peace.

For Bianca, her relationship with her beloved Jochen hadn't ended, it had changed. She was naturally devastated to not have his physical presence, but now she knew he was a part of her, and they were still connected. Her therapy sessions gave her a renewed sense of Jochen's strength, love, and presence – enough to help her to carry on.

Chapter 13

To Whom Much is Given, Much is Expected

I scanned the faces of the six doctors sitting around the u-shaped arrangement of tables in the hospital ward's meeting room. Still in protective Dad mode, I remained alert, questioning everything. I was utterly lost inside. Never in a million years did I expect I would be facing every parent's worst fear. Yet here we were.

Why so many doctors? I thought. I guess it's good that so many people are thinking about Jasper's case. Maybe then I wouldn't have to think so hard. A mix of devastation and exhaustion kept rolling knots around in my stomach. But as these experts trained in saving children's lives pulled their chairs in, adrenaline fuelled my focus.

One of the senior oncologists, Ben, was sitting on the right side of the room. Ben had a friendly face, with thin framed glasses and receding dark blonde hair. But this meeting was clearly serious, and he got straight to the point. Speaking deliberately, as if he was used to delivering important information to people, his tone was direct, and his words were clear. "We've got the results back from the last test, which we expected to confirm the provisional diagnosis," he started. "We now know it's definitely *not* what we thought it was."

What?

"We need to run another test," Ben continued, as I collected Jasper up from Annabel's arms. She'd been holding him for ages, trying to settle him. It was approaching time for his afternoon sleep and he was getting grizzly, but Annabel and I both needed to be in this meeting. "We now suspect the lump could be from a sub-type of tumours that are very responsive to treatment. We still need to get an exact diagnosis, but we are one step closer to knowing exactly what it is."

Did I hear that right? My head was spinning. Ever since the first hospital speculated on what they thought was wrong, everyone seemed to expect the provisional diagnosis would prove to be correct*. It seemed like just a matter of time before it was confirmed. I bounced Jasper gently up and down, letting the words settle in my mind. *Very responsive to treatment.*

Seated directly across from us was the senior surgeon, a kindly but serious looking man of Indian descent. "Shhh shhhh… this is good news," I said to Jasper before looking up and eyeballing the surgeon. I wanted to get a read on his face. His expression, still serious, gave way to gentle nod as he broke eye contact and looked down. He seemed hopeful, cautious, reserved.

We made arrangements for the next test to be done as soon as possible – later that afternoon – and made our way back to the ward to put Jasper down to sleep. It could be a few days before we would get the results. More waiting. Part of me was frustrated. Why was this so hard? Why so many doctors? We wanted answers. But there was something I desperately needed more than answers right now: hope. I started to feel a glimmer of hope. It had been a five-day waking

---

* I'm not mentioning the provisional diagnosis here because the specifics aren't necessary, and if someone's child has it, I don't want to add to their sense of alarm.

nightmare so far. No number of earnest reassurances that "we always aim for a cure" had stopped me from contemplating the worst. How on earth would we cope with *the worst*? I shoved those thoughts back whenever they arose. Intrusive thoughts of balloons and hearses and doves. What the fuck?! How did we get here? I wanted to scream! I wanted our old life back!

I wandered out into the corridor to take a breather from the rows of curtained hospital bays, like blue army tents in a warzone, with those words still swirling around my head... *very responsive to treatment*. One more test. Our baby boy had endured so many already. But we would do the test because this was a fight I couldn't contemplate losing. I felt adrenaline rushing through my body. Like a beaten down boxer finding energy to throw out another combination of punches when he sees a weakness in his opponent.

Lost in my daze I tuned out the bustle of the nurses' station, wandering aimlessly oblivious to the ringing phones, call bells, beeping machines, printers and chatter, when I saw Mum walking in through the double doors at the end of the corridor. She'd been steadfast in her support, coming in every day, usually twice a day. I knew she was hurting too, but she wanted to be there for us. As we reached each other and hugged I struggled to get my words out. My throat was choking up and I couldn't catch my breath. Tears had become so familiar I barely noticed them. After drawing a breath, I forced the words out with the urgency of throwing out a life buoy to someone lost at sea: "We have some hope."

That weekend was a blur, but I felt that hope rising in my heart. I tried not to think about the alternative. What if it was something even rarer? What if it was worse? It was late Monday afternoon when Ben came by the hospital room. "Can I come in?" he asked with a warm smile, poking his head around the door.

Jasper was sleeping, and Annabel was lying next to him in the hospital bed. "We've got the test results back, and we finally have a diagnosis." It was a strange sounding name that we got him to repeat a couple of times.

"Don't worry if you don't remember everything now. It's normal to forget some of what we talk about, and we'll have plenty of opportunities to go through it all again. You don't need to do anything right now, but tomorrow we'll go through the treatment plan. Now we know the exact protocol Jasper needs."

I wanted to get clear on what this all meant. Inside, part of me was hesitant, tentative. But I needed to know. "Ben, you mentioned in the meeting last week that it could be something very responsive to treatment. Is that what this is... the tumour type you were referring to?"

"Yes, it is." Ben spoke confidently and clearly, a manner that would become familiar in the coming months.

"So, this is good news?" I asked.

"It's *very* good news." Ben's tone was more relaxed now, but not casual. He understood the gravity of this moment. "You've got a tough few months ahead of you. But it's my expectation we will cure him."

The treatment regimen was on an outpatient basis, meaning we could live at home while Jasper was undergoing treatment, and visit the hospital for appointments. Still, the hospital became our second home. We got to know the doctors, nurses, and even the cleaners and orderlies. We'd swing open the fridge in the patient kitchen and pour apple juice with abandon or help ourselves to cheese and crackers. And we made a rule: anytime we went to the hospital we always went to the playground first. The Women's and Children's Hospital in Adelaide has a large courtyard on level 1, built into the middle of the building and directly under the flight path leading to Adelaide

International Airport. With fresh air and planes flying overhead, Jasper would smile and giggle as he slid down the slippery dip, unaware in that moment that he was in a hospital. His blue eyes would shine as he toddler-waddled around the play equipment, playing peak-a-boo or following bigger kids as they confidently climbed, jumped, and swung. The other rule was: after any procedure of any kind, we always got an ice cream. We didn't want Jasper to associate the hospital with bad things, and for the most part he didn't. He trusted us, and in return he amazed us with his ability to cope.

He was so brave and trusting. I realised this was partly Jasper's character but also a reflection of our loving bonds as a family. The pathology nurses were astonished every time, when patient after patient would scream and cry throughout their blood tests, then Jasper would watch calmly as they inserted the canula into his arm without so much as a whimper.

As much as we sheltered Jasper throughout this horribly unnatural experience, it was desperately stressful for Annabel and me. This battle tested us and changed us. Nobody spends any length of time on a children's cancer ward and remains the same. But our little family grew stronger. We relied on each other, trusted each other. We were there for each other in a thousand little ways over those weeks and months, both at hospital and at home. And boy did we need it, through the endless cycle of hospital visits and treatments and tests.

I was out in the garden one sunny morning when we got the phone call for the first blood results after treatment commenced. We needed Jasper's blood protein indicators to reduce to know the treatment was working. The numbers had dropped! We hung on to Ben's *very* good news, and trusted (and prayed) that we would get through this.

As best we could, we tried to resume some 'normal' parts of life. I had to work, and that often meant travel. My first trip away, to New

Zealand, was punishing. Three two-hour workshops a day, early morning flights, plus lunches and dinners with prospective business partners and clients. I oscillated between relief at having something else to focus on, to feeling like I would melt into a well of tears, to being consumed by an overwhelming, unrelenting, bone-deep exhaustion.

But nothing else mattered, other than those numbers going down.

Throughout it all, our love for Jasper shone. Still really just a baby, not even two years old, he was so unaware, unassuming, and always ready just to have fun and be loved. By the middle of the year, the numbers got so low that they were normal. As in, healthy normal. He was in remission! We just needed one more test, a scan, to determine whether all the cancer was gone.

The day we were due to get the results, I was driving, on my way home, praying. Always praying. Not in the hands clasped churchgoing kind of way, but more of a direct appeal to the mercy of God, the Universe, anything. I'd had enough spiritual experiences by now that I knew there was another side, a spiritual world that really exists, an actual place (or dimension) that we go to when we die. I knew there was a Creator. And I prayed to him each night, with a prayer I'd read in an old John Gray book:

Oh God, my heart is open to you. Please come sit in my heart.

Almost constantly, I prayed for Jasper's recovery. I have no idea whether my prayers made any difference. I'm certainly not claiming that they did because I can't possibly know for sure. But that day, two streets from home, praying to God as I drove, for the first time in my life I heard something back.

"He is healed."

It wasn't like someone was sitting next to me talking. I 'heard' it inside my head. The words came from outside of me but felt as though they reverberated through me. Strong, direct, and matter of fact. Stupefied, it's a wonder I didn't crash the car. I jerked the wheel slightly to the side and looked out at the rows of familiar family homes, fences and grassy verges, as if to remind myself I was really there. When I finally regained my senses, I was overcome.

"Thank you, thank you, thank you!"

The voice was completely without ego. It didn't claim responsibility for anything. The voice didn't say "I healed him." It was a simple statement in direct answer to my prayers. *He is healed.*

I kept the visit to myself. I couldn't help but feel self-doubt creeping in. Did I really hear that voice? Annabel was on enough of a rollercoaster without me adding another peak and risking another trough. Later that afternoon, the phone rang. Annabel and I huddled around her mobile on speaker mode like we had so many times before to hear Ben's kind, calm voice. But today was different. We hoped with every fibre of our being that this was finally the beginning of the end of our nightmare.

The scan was all clear.

We hugged and cried. We phoned our mums, 'the grandmas' who had been by our side through so many long days in hospital, hiding their tears, helping tend to our darling son, and keeping us going. Of course, there were months of tests to come. But Jasper was completely cancer free, and we could now focus on being on the other side of it.

"You said you believed you could cure him," I probed Ben during a subsequent hospital visit just before Christmas. "When would you say he is cured?"

"I believe he's already cured," Ben said in his familiar, direct manner. "We're just testing to make sure."

The testing, waiting, and worrying lasted years. Eventually, Ben said we didn't need to test anymore. It was now only serving a psychological function of reassurance for us. The tumour wasn't coming back.

For all the times I dreamt and imagined what life would feel like if we could get through this nightmare, I could only try to capture the feeling of relief and joy. But in reality, there's never a full stop. You don't go back to being your old self. You don't celebrate recovery from cancer like you would a lotto win. It's better than a lotto win, without question, but it feels more like a soldier who's been in the trenches coming home from a war: immense relief, exhaustion, hypervigilance, and hoping like hell you never have to face the horror of battle again. You are also forever tainted by the realisation that horrible shit can happen to you and those you love.

My fear of dying from all those years ago, when Nanna failed to reassure me in the laundry, was long gone. But this brush with death wasn't about my own death. It was worse. Marriage and fatherhood had brought a new fear to bear: fear of the death of those I love the most. I've read so many NDE testimonies that I know dying is beautiful. Yet knowing death is a peaceful, painless, and even ecstatic experience didn't stop my fear of losing a loved one. I don't suppose it would for anyone. We want them here, not there.

My wilful ignorance of assuming bad things don't happen to people like us had shattered like a chandelier on a marble floor. You never quite return to the person you were before. You can't step back into a world where your deepest fears seem so unlikely that they don't really exist, they aren't in your everyday consciousness. That part of your awareness, scarred by the wounds of reality, always knows disaster could strike. You can't live anticipating it – because that ruins everything – but the possibility is now always there.

I thought often of the families we met in the hospital. We knew their pain. We recognised the familiar stress and worry in their eyes, and the unbelievable strength of love that dominates every waking moment caring for your sick child. That some of them would not have the fortunate outcome we did was heartbreaking.

We were so very fortunate. This meant the aftermath of our trauma was accompanied by something sublime: gratitude. If there's a spiritual reason behind the painful events of our lives, designed to help us evolve, then this was its gift: not ever taking for granted the magic and love in the mundane routines of family life. The minor irritations that had bothered me before, the self-centred concerns that so distracted me from what really mattered – all of that melted away.

Our toddler quickly turned into a boy. We relished his personality, his health, and our experiences as a family. Each day I would stop, catching myself in a moment of utter normality, marvelling at its return. Normal, boring, everyday life was what we dreamed of and hoped for back in those dark days. Now we rejoiced in the normality we feared we'd never get to see again. I simply couldn't, mustn't, and wouldn't forget our good fortune.

As life resumed with our healthy boy growing up blissfully unaware of the emotional bruising and trauma carried by his parents, my thoughts turned back to IADC. Given what my family had been through, and the horrible outcome we'd so narrowly avoided, if I could in some way heal the pain of those who suffered devastating grief and yet chose not to, could I live with that? Like a persistent gaze, this thought bore down on me day and night. I tried to shrug it off. Anyone who's been through a trauma knows how powerful the pull of avoidance is. I just wanted to feel some peace again. To relax a little and try to resume my normal life. I didn't want to think about it. Had I forgotten that suppressing thoughts doesn't work?

Lying in bed at night the thought persisted, withholding sleep, demanding I confront it. I knew IADC therapy could dramatically reduce the sadness and pain of grief. The fear of judgement and excuses about timing didn't carry much weight anymore. Not in the context of how it could help those whose loved ones *had* died. Could

I then, in good conscience, withhold this help from those who endured the fate I had dreaded more than anything? Torn between immense gratitude and relief, I still held a fear of Jasper dying that haunted me. Then I'd feel ashamed for indulging my fear when there were other families out there whose children hadn't made it. Who am I to complain when my son's own doctor says he is cured? God (or at least *someone* in the spiritual realm) even told me he is cured! Still, every fibre of my being wanted to run as far away as I could from hospitals, sickness, grief, and death. I wanted to slam that door shut and throw away the key!

I tossed and turned in tangled bedsheets as I contemplated the mission before me. First, I'd need to fly to Chicago to train in IADC therapy with Dr Botkin. Then, I'd need to conduct research to establish its scientific credibility. This was the next logical step. I'd heard Dr Botkin say in podcast interviews that they needed university research like a controlled trial, to get it out into mainstream psychology. Finally, I would provide it to grieving people around the world. I'd be slaying my own demons by helping others.

I thought about those long days with Jasper and Annabel in hospital, and the long dark nights with me in the Air B&B up the road. It felt like I was bargaining with God. Then I realised how stupidly self-important it was to bargain with God. I wasn't in control! After all the tears, all the wishing, all the prayers, I had been spared grief. And now I was to bring healing to those who stared into the abyss of grief. I didn't just feel obligated, I was *compelled*.

This was my covenant with God.

Not a bargain, a covenant. A sacred promise. It is what I must do. Reverence overcame me as I finally acknowledged and accepted this part of my life's purpose. I inhaled deeply and pulled up the sheets once more as sweat cooled on my brow, letting out a long, slow breath as I contemplated the mission I'd just committed to. Gratitude welled up within me. Thankfully, courage, too, came with it. I'd have to stare death in the face again and again if I was going to be a grief therapist. In time, I would learn that by using IADC therapy to bring light into the darkness of deep sadness and loss I was forging a protective layer around my own heart, and slowly reaching closer to the spirit of the divine. In the still silence of the dark, I reached out once again to the spiritual world:

Oh God, my heart shines for you. Thank you for being in my heart.

Chapter 14

Monica

When I first spoke to Monica, a young mum of two with a bright smile and brown hair, she described August as "death month". She'd had so many deaths in the month of August – from her grandpa to other relatives and even her beloved pet dog – it felt like a curse her family couldn't escape. She always felt dread in the pit of her stomach when August rolled around, in anticipation of who might die next.

But even more intriguing than her purported family curse, Monica had herself died before! And yes – it was in August!

Monica was getting ready to go on a date when a friend called in to see her. As she greeted him at the door, she suddenly had a coughing fit. She ran to her bedroom to get her water bottle when she collapsed. Monica was having a cardiac arrest. Her friend attempted CPR until paramedics arrived to find her without a pulse. After delivering seven shocks with a defibrillator and three rounds of adrenaline in a desperate attempt to bring her back to life, she was finally loaded into the ambulance with less than one percent chance of survival. Nobody expected her to last the night.

Monica recalled, "My first memory was waking up in the cardiac ward and seeing my dad sitting in front of the window. I knew I was in hospital, but I had no idea why. I couldn't remember anything, and because my ribs and sternum were broken, I thought I'd been in a car accident."

Monica had to learn to swallow, talk, walk, and care for herself and her kids again. She told me that despite how far she's come, she still experiences memory loss and fatigue today. But it was what happened when Monica was 'gone' that made her so intriguing to me as a grief client: she had an NDE.

Monica described many of the hallmarks of a classic NDE when she 'died': swirling lights and colours, an incredible sense of peace and wellbeing, and sensing the presence of a deceased loved one. In fact, it was the very loved one she sensed in her NDE that Monica was grieving: her beloved nanna, "Rose".

Rose was a real character. She had a cheeky personality, never taking things too seriously. "She was always laughing and making light of the situation, no matter how bad it was," Monica told me. "I felt like she was my main caregiver growing up. Dad was away with the army a lot. I just felt like she was my parental figure. I think that helped with our closeness as well. Growing up was just fun. Everyone said I had her wrapped around my little finger. She would go to the shops to buy us ice blocks, but when we'd walk back, I would want to go to the park to play on the play equipment. She'd say, 'Bloody hell, Monny, I've got ice blocks!' But we'd end up sitting at the park because that's what I wanted to do. We'd end up eating the whole box of ice blocks at the park because they weren't going to make it home without melting."

I couldn't help but think of my Nanna. This is exactly the kind of thing she'd do! If I wanted ice cream, she'd get it. If I wanted to go somewhere and play, we'd do it. I never quite thought of it as having her wrapped around my little finger, but I realise now that's a perfect way of putting it. I couldn't help but smile.

My ADC with Nanna had given me such peace, and marked the beginning of a real sense of reconnection with her. Scribbling on my notepad as Monica spoke, I thought about how much I wanted that for her too. It was when I asked her to tell me about Rose's death that I could see how deeply it affected her.

"She collapsed at the bus stop. Someone at the bus stop rang an ambulance and she got taken to hospital. As far as we knew, she was going to get some fluids and then be sent home later that day or the next day." But the more tests they did, it seemed the more things they found that were wrong with her. Despite relentless blood transfusions and even more tests, the doctors finally said there wasn't much more they could do. "In the end she said, 'give the blood to someone else who needs it, it isn't helping', and she declined all treatment. She died four days later."

The night Rose died, Monica had spent most of the day in hospital with her, and it was late at night when she left. Soon after going to bed, Monica got the phone call saying Rose was gone. "We expected her to go for another two days, but she just went like that." Monica clicked her fingers. "So that was probably rock bottom. I had to change my ring tone on my phone."

The ring tone she associated with the phone call to tell her that Rose had died, continued to trigger intense fear and panic in Monica even years later. This is what psychologists call 're-experiencing symptoms' as a result of traumatic stress: it feels as if the traumatic event is happening again.

Not only did Rose's death cause Monica immense sadness, but it was also a source of guilt. You see, Rose's fun-loving ways had a downside: she had become addicted to alcohol. In her final years, she lived off tinned soup and canned vegetables and wasn't taking good care of herself. Monica wished she had done more. "She did so much for me growing up, when I didn't have the typical mum and dad life.

She was an alcoholic, and I feel guilty that I should have been firmer with her."

I started the bilateral stimulation by tapping gently on the back of Monica's hands as they rested on her knees while she had her eyes closed: left, right, left, right. The initial target was her strongest piece of sadness: the phone call. "Don't try to manage it at all, just see what happens to the sadness as we go," I said as she closed her eyes.

After only the fourth set of bilateral stimulation, Monica opened her eyes and told me what she'd noticed. It was clear that things were moving very quickly. "Bright colours. Like this vivid pink colour... and words... but I couldn't make out the words," she said. Seeing vivid colours was a sign an ADC was unfolding.

"And how did you feel emotionally?" I asked, knowing that the unfolding of an ADC is always met with good feelings.

"Calm."

The rapid progress we were making with bilateral stimulation astounded me. We were only ten minutes in, and she was already in a receptive state. I had to pivot. It wasn't about the sadness anymore; I sensed a connection with Rose was coming. "Now just think about Rose in a general way and just go with whatever happens," I instructed. Two sets later Monica reported she was feeling happiness.

"Is that happiness related to Rose?" I asked.

"Yeah."

"What would you want to say to Rose if you could?"

"We always talked about death and the afterlife, and if there is one. And she always said that if ever she died, or if I died, we'd meet each other at the gate, to go on together. And then when I had my near-death experience, I could see the kids floating off to my left, lots of colours in a beautiful stream in front of me, and then to my right I had a big door. But it was shut and there was nobody there to meet me." Monica seemed surprised and somewhat confused that although she had *felt* Rose's presence in her NDE, she didn't actually *see* Rose.

After another set of tapping, Monica opened her eyes with surprise.

"Fuck! I thought I heard her saying she couldn't be there for me because it wasn't my time."

I resumed tapping and asked Monica to close her eyes again. As I tapped on her hands, I noticed subtle changes in her facial expression. After a couple of minutes, she opened her eyes. "Wow. That was really cool!" Monica exclaimed.

"What did you notice?" I asked.

"I could see her writing 'Monny, I love you'. I got the *feeling* that she was telling me that had she been there, I would have gone to her. And then I would have not been there for the kids."

Despite things moving so fast in this session, Monica was very matter of fact about her new insights. I wondered whether her earlier NDE meant she was already open to whatever would unfold. She wasn't hesitant at all. She wasn't judging every little sensation as it occurred.

"So, that's why she wasn't there," Monica explained. "Because I would have run to her and then the door's shut and I can't come back. That makes sense with her saying 'It wasn't your time to be here'. She knew I would have run to her, and then I'd have left the kids. Wow."

Monica sighed as she leant back in the red chair. Her nanna had been there for her during her cardiac arrest, but she needed to stay out of sight. It had bothered Monica for so long that she hadn't been able to see Rose in that moment, but now a big weight had been lifted. "I feel a lot better. People could have said that to me, to comfort me, but now I have heard the explanation from Rose herself."

Monica also noticed that when she tried to recall some of the distressing memories of Rose in hospital, they now felt different. It was not uncommon for IADC clients to notice that distressing memories fade, feel more distant, or have a new emotion attached. "I'm feeling happier," Monica said with a surprised tone. "I can see her in hospital now – in my memory – but it feels more like a happy memory, not so doom and gloom. Wow."

Now I wanted Monica to have the chance to resolve any outstanding issues or concerns she might have had regarding her relationship with Rose. "Is there anything you wanted to say to her? You mentioned earlier there is a piece of sadness around... you said you felt a bit guilty that you weren't tougher on her, with the drinking, or looking after her with her eating, or things like that. Shall we do a set starting from there and see what happens?"

Monica agreed. She opened her eyes about thirty seconds after I stopped tapping.

"I had a revelation that she would've done it anyway," she said with a quiet certainty, referring to Rose's excessive drinking. "It makes so much sense. She was very determined. By God, if she wanted alcohol, she would have frigging crawled down to the Bottle-O and gotten some. She still would have been able to do it. Because I wouldn't have been able to stay with her 24/7. She would have gone out after dark. She didn't care. She's getting alcohol. Yeah, nobody would dare mess with her."

This was a crucial insight for Monica. She'd carried guilt for years, but in a moment, the guilt seemed to melt away.

"Is there anything else you wanted to ask Rose, or say to her, or anything else we should address now?" I asked. When a connection is established, I want to ensure the client has plenty of opportunity to resolve any lingering questions or concerns.

"I guess just giving her a hug and telling her that I miss her, but that I'm okay."

"Let's go with that," I said as she closed her eyes again and I started tapping on her hands.

"Wow. God, I could smell her! I could smell her and feel her bear hug," Monica said with eyes wide in amazement at what she was experiencing.

"So, you got your hug?" I smiled.

"Yeah. Wow. She used to give these bear hugs that'd crack your back. For an old lady she was bloody strong! It was just an enveloping feeling of 'It's okay, I'm here'".

"How's your sadness now?" I asked.

Monica seemed to be scanning herself before she answered. "I don't know if I feel sad anymore," she said, thoughtful but surprised. "Like... I feel happy that I get to hear that message from her; it makes a lot of sense that she wasn't there for me in my NDE, because it wasn't my time. But she'll be with me when it is my time. It feels like a big revelation."

On the second day of our therapy sessions, I could already see a lightness in Monica as she recounted her experience from the day before. She'd slept well, and even after one session, she was able to talk about Rose without such sadness. She told me she felt more accepting, like everything had happened for a reason.

"So yesterday you moved into the receptive state very quickly," I said as I deciphered my scribbled hand-written notes. "We did 11 sets of bilateral stimulation... after four, you reported seeing colours and feeling calm, then it was followed by feeling peaceful, seeing Rose, hearing her voice, feeling a hug, and smelling her... so you've had all these sensory experiences in one." It was truly remarkable how many different types of ADC Monica had experienced in one session.

"Where you got to by the end of yesterday is really where we aim to get people by the end of the second day," I told her. The fact that she'd previously had an NDE could be the reason, I mused. Perhaps she was already somehow connected to the other side. I asked Monica if any new pieces of sadness had arisen.

She answered, "Just… why haven't I been able to experience something like this any earlier? Because it would have saved me a lot of years of stress and shit!"

A lot of people say that after their IADC therapy: I wish I'd had this sooner. I asked her to scan herself for any remaining sadness directly related to Rose's death.

"We thought we'd have longer", she said.

"Alright, go back to that feeling of 'we thought we'd have longer'. Let yourself feel whatever emotion goes along with that, and then we'll just do some more tapping," I instructed.

Just as the day before, the processing moved quickly, and she felt Rose's presence.

"I could hear her say that she thought she had more time too." After a pause, Monica added: "She's happy where she is." I continued with sets of tapping on the back of her hands.

"I feel warm and cozy. It's nice."

"Emotionally, how do you feel?" I asked.

"Just calm about everything."

"And did you notice anything specific about Rose or Rose's presence then?" I probed.

"Like… happiness. Like a happy presence."

"That *she* is happy?" I questioned.

"Yeah."

As we tapped, Monica had another profound realisation about her grandmother's passing. "I've gotten to hear her say what she said, and feel her hugs, and just smell her and stuff. It's like I've had that closure. It's like a resolution," she reflected. "It's like I still miss her, but it's not like a deep-down-in-my-heart pain. I feel lighter now."

By the end of our time together, Monica had reached a place of peace and acceptance. "I feel like I've gotten what I need. Like I've got that closure and acceptance of her," she stated with conviction. "I'll always miss her, but I don't have that sadness attached to her… It's like I've understood everything." The relief was evident in her voice.

In just two ninety-minute sessions, Monica had achieved the very thing so many grieving people long for – a sense of resolution, understanding, and the ability to remember her beloved relative with love rather than overwhelming pain. Her grief had been transformed from intense sadness into peace and acceptance. Their bond continued to exist, but with different emotions attached, freeing Monica to move forward with lightness.

As we ended our final session, I couldn't help but feel a deep sense of gratitude for the gift of being able to facilitate such profound healing. Monica's transformation was a testament to the power of IADC therapy and the in-built healing ability we all have within our bodies, brains, and spirit. It also reflected the transformative power of NDEs. Monica spent no time questioning whether connecting to a deceased relative was possible. She wasn't apprehensive about the idea of anything unusual happening. She was simply open and ready. There's no question in my mind that this was why she was able to enter a receptive state so quickly, and her openness rewarded her with all manner of ADC phenomena.

And just as I got to experience a life-changing ADC with my Nanna, I was able to help Monica have one with her nanna too.

I emailed Monica six months later, to check in and see how she was going, and to ask if I could include her story in this book. She replied immediately, and was still feeling the benefits of her IADC:

I certainly felt lighter and more free after my sessions with you and it's funny, I can think about Rose now but I'm not feeling that achy, mournful feeling of missing her. I still miss her, but I'm happy I had her in my life as closely as I did for as long as I did.

Chapter 15

Science Meets Spirit

On the 23rd December, 2021, I was lazing on my bed while Annabel and Jasper packed their bags for our Christmas getaway to the beach house. I would always pack at the last minute and usually forget something. I was happy to drag my feet. It was that time of year when I'd finally get a moment to draw breath, focus on things other than day-to-day work, and start thinking about my plans and goals for the year ahead. IADC therapy was on my mind.

I'd made my silent promise and was committed to deliver on it. I'd already done my EMDR training, which was interesting but uneventful. I thought it was amazing that bilateral stimulation (through eye movement, tapping, or other methods) was seemingly 100% successful in reducing distress in clients to *at least some degree*. Of course, I didn't want to treat trauma in the way mainstream EMDR was designed, I wanted to heal grief and help people reconnect with their lost loved ones as Dr Botkin described. But the COVID pandemic was in full swing which delayed everything. I was forced into biding my time. I'd always assumed that getting trained in IADC therapy would require me to make the almost 24 hours of flight time to get to Chicago to see Dr Botkin personally.

As I scrolled absentmindedly on my phone lying on the bed, something caught my attention: an email from the mailing list of Sandra Champlain, host of the *We Don't Die* podcast (the podcast on which I'd first heard about Dr Botkin and IADC therapy). Botkin's name jumped out at me from the text. Something about a documentary film on healing grief.

Wait. What?

A new feature film documentary had been produced and was available to watch, pre-release, through a private online screening for *We Don't Die* listeners!

That night in our little beach house at Port Willunga, I watched *Life With Ghosts* for the first time, and was mesmerised. The film tells the story of several widowed ladies living in a retirement community in Florida, and their attempts to deal with their grief. One character, Irene, feels comforted when she perceives the presence of her late husband through happenings such as flickering lights in her living room. But these experiences are promptly dismissed by her grief counsellor and a psychiatrist who even interrogates her for drug use![17]

The stories of these women are brilliantly woven together to reveal the comfort of after-death communication. The film also introduces a research study evaluating IADC therapy at the University of North Texas[18]. Professor Jan Holden was the lead investigator (and already one of the world's foremost authorities on NDEs and related phenomena, and someone I admired immensely). Not only has she published extensively in scientific journals, she is also a licensed professional counsellor, counsellor educator, IADC practitioner, and president of IANDS.

Watching Professor Holden's research in action, seeing the impact the therapy had on participants, and the heartwarming conclusion of the film, pushed a button inside me. I switched off the TV screen and sat back in the dark in awe. This is what I'm meant to be doing, I thought. If I have to fly to Chicago, I will. It was now or never. Before I went to bed, I sent Dr Botkin an email.

In the morning, I had his reply. He was retired now, he told me. But I could get trained online! He recommended I contact César Valdez, which I did immediately. Two months later, under the excellent tutelage of César (who would go on to be a great mentor), I was a certified IADC therapist!

There's one question aching in the heart of any grieving person: *'Is the afterlife real?'* It was a question my 8-year-old brain could not yet conceive of when I anxiously questioned Nanna in the laundry. But years later I would have an answer. The afterlife is real, there is no death, our loved ones are not gone, and we will be reunited with them again.

However, one of the greatest obstacles to embracing these profound experiences is the pervasive influence of scientism – the belief that science is the sole arbiter of truth and that only phenomena that are directly observable, measurable, and repeatable in laboratory settings are worthy of serious consideration. This strictly materialistic worldview dismisses subjective experiences like NDEs and ADCs and limits our understanding of the full spectrum of human experience.

I can't prove to you that NDEs and ADCs are real, any more than you can prove that you dream. But I know it's true, just like you know what chocolate ice-cream tastes like, or what it feels like to love someone deeply. These are all subjective experiences. Social scientists have relied on subjective self-report data for eons to learn much about humans and our worldly experiences. It might be the kind of science that a mathematician or engineer would sneer at, but it is science, nonetheless.

Empiricism is the theory that all knowledge is based on experience derived from the senses. As such, empirical evidence relates to data obtained by observation and experience. True empiricism, in the context of justification for belief in an afterlife, is the acquisition of knowledge from direct experience and observation – precisely the kind of data near-death experiencers provide when they share their experiences.

Where one or two similar stories can be dismissed as mere anecdotes, if hundreds or thousands of stories have similar defining features, it becomes compelling empirical data. These data are now made available by scientists, presented in a scientific way, asking scientific questions, and confronting the dismissal of critics whose materialist worldview demands they reject these life-changing phenomena out of hand.

By recognising the limitations imposed by scientism, we can open ourselves to a more integrative approach. One that honours both the rigour of scientific inquiry and the rich tapestry of subjective, spiritual experiences that reveal much about the nature of our existence.

One such scientific endeavour is the collection of many thousands of cases of NDEs and ADCs by Dr Jeff and Jody Long, with their extraordinary database of evidence for the afterlife at nderf.org and adcrf.org. Personal testimonies from around the world, written in the words and style of the experiencer, of varying lengths and detail, describe an innumerable variety of circumstances in which people have had NDEs. Yet despite these variations, incredible consistencies emerge. And sometimes, respected scientists and health and medical professionals observe and experience phenomena that contravene mainstream scientific explanations. Some of them have gone on to conduct scientific research of their own, collating further evidence for what exists on the other side of death.

As a resident psychiatrist in the 1970's, Dr Bruce Greyson was caring for a young woman who had attempted suicide. His first job after eating a spaghetti lunch and spilling some of the sauce on his tie, was to interview the woman in question. But when he attended her room, she was unconscious, so he had to return later. When the patient was awake and Dr Greyson returned, albeit with a clean tie, she remarked about the spaghetti stain from the previous visit. She described having left her body and observing the comings and goings of her hospital room from a vantage point on the ceiling. Greyson's spaghetti-stain-on-the-tie story was not only compelling empirical evidence that consciousness is not limited to our bodies, it was a turning point in Greyson's career as it spurred him to become a leading authority on near-death and related phenomena (see his excellent book *After: A Doctor Explores What Near-Death Experiences Reveal About Life and Beyond*[19].) If respected medical doctors and scientists take near-death phenomena seriously, why shouldn't the broader scientific community?

Likewise, cardiologist Dr. Mike Sabom also became a keen investigator into afterlife phenomena. When a colleague presented him with Raymond Moody's seminal book on NDEs, *Life After Life*, he denounced it as "hogwash". With a belief set grounded in medical science, he was uninterested in such phenomena until a colleague encouraged him to ask patients he had resuscitated about their experiences. "The third one I talked to gave me a textbook picture of the near-death experience just as Moody had written about in his book *Life After Life*."[20]

Dr Sabom conducted a groundbreaking five-year study, detailed in his own book *Light and Death: One Doctor's Fascinating Account of Near-Death Experiences*[21], involving 160 participants and amassing over 3,000 data points. Sabom was particularly interested in the 'autoscopic' experiences – where people claimed to have left their bodies and observed their own resuscitation. Of the 30 such cases he found, six stood out as remarkably detailed and potentially verifiable. Ever the rigorous scientist, Dr Sabom insisted on third-party verification or medical documents to corroborate these accounts. He categorized experiences into autoscopic (seeing from another vantage point), transcendental (involving tunnels, lights, and deceased relatives), or a combination of both. Crucially, Sabom highlighted the paradox of these experiences: "During a cardiac arrest your brain waves are flat in 15 seconds. With flat brain waves you're not able to perceive visually anything with your physical eyes, and these people were telling me what they were seeing."

This observation challenged the conventional understanding of consciousness and its relationship to brain activity. In fact, it shatters the assumption that consciousness is caused by brain activity and the oft-cited claim that NDE phenomena are a result of brain activity in a dying brain.

Dr Sabom also provided the NDE literature with one of the most compelling cases ever recorded: the NDE of Pam Reynolds. In 1991, Pam Reynolds was diagnosed with a life-threatening brain aneurysm. Her only hope was a daring operation called a "standstill" procedure. Essentially, the surgeons needed to stop Pam's heart and drain the blood from her brain, reducing her body temperature to a frigid 15.5°C – the equivalent of induced clinical death. This would allow them to delicately remove the aneurysm without rupturing it. To ensure her eyes didn't dry out during the lengthy operation, they were securely taped shut. Moulded ear speakers played rapid clicks at a loud 95 decibels, monitoring her brain stem's response to sound, to confirm total inactivity. Pam, by all medical standards, was as dead as one could be while still being able to be revived. Yet, she later recounted vivid details of the procedure, including conversations among the medical staff and the saw used to cut open her skull, which she described as looking like an "electric toothbrush". Pam further reported a journey through a tunnel, encounters with deceased loved ones, and a brilliant light. The implications were staggering: despite having no measurable brain activity, Pam experienced a complex, lucid adventure seemingly outside her physical body. Dr. Sabom, meticulous in his documentation, considers Pam's case to be "the number one best documented case on record". For those seeking evidence that consciousness can exist beyond the brain, Pam Reynolds' story is as close to proof as it gets.

My own experience of consciousness existing beyond my physical body came unexpectedly in the early hours of the morning at our beach house in Port Willunga. With my body sound asleep in bed, I suddenly become fully alert and aware, flying over the clifftops of Silver Sands and Aldinga Beach. With crystal clear vision I surveyed the sandy brown and green sandhills as I flew, exhilarated with a feeling of complete freedom, wellbeing, and wonderment. The familiar expanse of water seemed so much larger from my perspective up high, while the world below was illuminated by a kind of azure glow. I couldn't tell if it was coming from the reflection of the stars on the calm ocean or emanating from the environment itself. In total, my out of body experience lasted less than a minute before I jolted back into my body, marvelling at the journey and soaking in the tingly vibrations and pleasant waves of energy coursing through me.

Any remnants of my childhood fear of death finally dissipated with three things: experiencing myself fully conscious outside of my body; my experience of reconnection with my grandparents in my three spontaneous ADCs; and the abundance of empirical evidence that not only do we survive death but the hereafter is joyful, peaceful, and feels more like home than anything we experience in this physical life.

Those who don't believe in the survival of consciousness from bodily death have often argued that NDEs are products of a dying brain: that neurochemicals, hypoxia, medications, and many other spurious physiological or psychological causes are behind these consistently transformative experiences. Anything, except the afterlife being real. Dr Sabom's work transformed him from a sceptic who initially dismissed NDEs as hogwash to a leading authority in the field, demonstrating that even the most scientifically minded could find compelling evidence in these extraordinary experiences, when the brain should be incapable of producing them.

Empirical data from thousands of cases, meticulously documented by researchers like Dr. Bruce Greyson, Dr. Mike Sabom, and Prof. Jan Holden, reveal a phenomenon far too consistent and coherent to be dismissed as a neurochemical glitch. From the peaceful feelings to the encounters with deceased loved ones, these experiences follow remarkably similar patterns across cultures, ages, and belief systems. And let's not forget the transformative impact on those who've been there – even die-hard sceptics have emerged from NDEs with a newfound conviction in the afterlife.

Moreover, NDEs stand in stark contrast to the typical characteristics of hallucinations. While hallucinations are often disjointed, erratic, unpleasant, incoherent, and lacking in meaning, NDEs are known for their clarity, coherence, and profound significance. The overwhelming majority of near-death experiencers report experiences that are not only lucid and organised but also imbued with a deep sense of meaning and insight.

But perhaps the most compelling evidence lies in the details. Experiencers often recount vivid, verifiable perceptions from their out-of-body adventures – things they couldn't possibly have known or seen from their hospital bed. And then there are cases like Pam Reynolds, where the NDE occurred during a period of clinically-monitored brain death. Try as they might, the "dying brain" theorists can't explain away these inconvenient truths. The hallucination hypothesis, once a cornerstone of NDE scepticism, is crumbling under the weight of empirical evidence. As science (not scientism) continues to illuminate the mysteries of consciousness, it's becoming increasingly clear that the afterlife isn't just a comforting myth – it's a reality waiting for us all. Some of the most compelling evidence comes from cases where near-death experiencers receive verifiable information they couldn't possibly have known through ordinary means.

There are many well-known veridical accounts within the NDE literature – those that are verifiably true. A good example of these kind of cases is that of Ray Feurstein, who was only a teenager getting ready for his prom when his appendix burst[22]. He experienced many of the classic NDE features such as bright lights and a feeling of peace and wellbeing. But then he was approached by a woman wearing a blue stone pendant, claiming to be his grandmother (someone he had never met as she died before he was born). She told him he couldn't stay, but "please tell your mom that you met me, and I said to say hello, and everything is fine, and also tell her that Tommy is good, he's doing well.'"

After two weeks in the hospital, Ray finally got to properly share his experience with his mother. He related the story of this kind lady claiming to be his grandmother, with the blue pendant: "She says tell your mother that everything is fine here and Tommy is doing well." Once his mother returned to her senses after initially looking shocked and dumbfounded, she ran upstairs to return with the blue pendant necklace he'd seen in his NDE. When Ray asked who Tommy was, his mother confessed that it was Ray's younger brother who died. Ray had never heard about Tommy prior to his NDE.

The gathering evidence of various research studies and documented cases suggest that the brain doesn't produce consciousness, it inhibits it. Pim Van Lommel is a Dutch cardiologist who conducted one of the largest hospital-based studies of NDEs, published in the prestigious medical journal *The Lancet*[23]. He suggests that the brain is a filter or receiver, like a TV or radio. What we perceive as reality, Van Lommel argues, is just a narrow band of a much vaster spectrum of consciousness. During an NDE, when brain function is impaired, that filter is lifted, allowing access to an expanded awareness normally hidden from us. It's a radical idea, but one that makes sense of the profound experiences reported by near-death experiencers. If consciousness is indeed fundamental to our nature and the brain merely a conduit, then it's no surprise that phenomenal experiences can occur even when the brain is offline.

Van Lommel's work also highlights the transformative power of NDEs. Many of his subjects reported profound changes in their attitudes, beliefs, and values after their brush with death. For them, the NDE wasn't just a bizarre neurological glitch – it was a spiritual awakening, a glimpse behind the veil that separates this life from the next. I wondered whether the 'receptive state' in IADC therapy was also an example of opening the receiver to a broader spectrum of experience.

It's no surprise that Dr. Raymond Moody, the pioneering psychiatrist who coined the term 'near-death experience' and wrote the international bestseller *Life After Life*, also took a keen interest in after-death communications. He studied an ancient Greek method of 'conjuring the dead' through a specially equipped room known as a psychomanteum. In it, clients would peer into the black depths of a mirror, positioned such that the client could not see themselves, but simply the inky depth of a black curtain behind them, with only a candle or dim light to illuminate the space[24].

Dr. Moody found that this setup facilitated powerful emotional experiences for many participants. In the psychomanteum, some individuals reported vivid encounters with departed loved ones, often describing these as deeply healing and cathartic. While not everyone experienced a visual manifestation, many felt a profound sense of connection through auditory impressions, emotional communication, or a heightened sense of presence. Occasionally, participants perceived the deceased to step out of the mirror and communicate directly.

Dr. Moody theorised that the psychomanteum created a state of altered consciousness, akin to those found in NDEs, which allowed the mind to bypass ordinary barriers of perception. This ancient ritual, reimagined for modern times, offered clients an opportunity to process unresolved grief and find comfort in the possibility of continued connection with those who had passed on. Dr Moody's facilitated reunions with lost loved ones was a pioneering form of after-death communication therapy.

Of course, Van Lommel and Moody's ideas aren't without controversy. Materialist scientists argue that there must be some as-yet-undiscovered physical mechanism behind NDEs and ADCs. But as the evidence mounts, their objections ring increasingly hollow. The implications of these research projects are profound: they challenge the very foundations of what we've been told to believe about the nature of reality.

Another phenomenon that challenges the idea of consciousness being intrinsic to the brain is terminal lucidity: when old, frail, and extremely ill patients on their deathbed suddenly re-animate to converse lucidly with loved ones, when they had been comatose or unable to speak for weeks or months prior. Only recently have scientists begun to investigate this phenomenon which has been documented – and ridiculed – for centuries.

Dr Alexander Batthyány, a Hungarian researcher, has collected compelling evidence of this phenomenon in his recent book *Threshold: Terminal lucidity and the border between life and death*[25]. The book features several striking cases, such as that of Anna Katharina Ehmer, a severely disabled girl who had never spoken a single word in her life. Yet, just hours before her death, she began to sing fluently, astounding her family. Another case Batthyány cites is that of a 92-year-old woman with advanced Alzheimer's who, in the days leading up to her death, suddenly started having lucid conversations with her family, despite not having recognised them for years.

These cases, and others like them, pose a significant challenge to the notion that consciousness is solely a product of brain activity. In someone with advanced Alzheimer's, the brain basically shrivels and shrinks. The parts that handle memory and thinking just waste away. If the brain is so severely compromised by disease or age, and if consciousness is produced or dependent upon the brain, how can such sudden clarity emerge right before death? If instead consciousness is non-local, that is, it operates beyond the boundaries of our physical brain and even beyond space and time, then terminal lucidity is just one of many natural, understandable phenomena reflecting the notion that we exist beyond the physical.

Of all these related phenomena, the science of after-death communication is the most compelling, to me, because when it occurs through the IADC therapy protocol it provides a repeatable, therapeutic application for healing grief. As you now know, ADCs are very common, and have been studied seriously in various ways including:

- A 1971 study by Dewy Rees who conducted a survey of widows and widowers in Wales, finding that 47% of them had ADCs[26]
- The Guggenheims' case study research involving over 3,300 cases, which established a picture of ADCs as a natural, common and healing phenomenon.[4]
- A survey in Iceland that revealed 31% of the general population had ADCs.[27]

Currently, a major collaboration in Europe, between Swiss researcher Evelyn Elsaesser and her colleagues from the University of Northampton, has surveyed over 1000 ADC experiencers in three languages[28].

Unfortunately, some researchers and practitioners still tend to pathologise the experience – just as the social worker and psychiatrist did in *Life With Ghosts* – despite mounting evidence that these are overwhelmingly described as positive experiences. For this reason, we need to do more research to clarify the nature of ADCs, and in particular their therapeutic benefits. This is where *Induced* After Death Communication comes in.

As my growing passion for IADC therapy led me to scouring the research literature, I came across something that stopped me in my tracks: a case of an induced ADC that *predates* Botkin. Where Dr Botkin discovered IADC in 1995, he didn't publish a paper on his discovery until 2000[29]. Yet in the 1996 edition (volume 28, number 2) of the *Journal of Transpersonal Psychology*, clinical psychologist Dr Laurel Parnell wrote an article called *Eye movement desensitization and reprocessing (EMDR) and spiritual unfolding*[30]. She described how EMDR can generate feelings of peace and love, as well as spiritual insights, and described a case in which she was treating a bereaved person and focused on – you guessed it – sadness:

> *[A client] had survived a devastating fire which killed several women students in her college dorm. After EMDR processing of this event for about fifteen minutes, she reported much relief – but still felt a great deal of sadness. So I requested that she stay with the sadness and continue the eye movements even though she thought she had processed it as far as it would go.*
>
> *After a few minutes she reported experiencing an image in which all of the women in the school had formed a circle and held hands. The women who had died slowly floated up into*

the sky as they danced happily. The client felt great peace and happiness with this imagery and remained with a feeling of closure with this issue.

Remarkably, ADCs were induced in a therapeutic manner, using modified EMDR, independently, by two clinical psychologists at around the same time. Dr Parnell wasn't trying to induce an ADC, but by focusing on the sadness and continuing with eye movements beyond when standard EMDR would stop, an ADC occurred, and it healed the client. Dr Botkin, of course, deserves immense credit for recognising the specific elements of the process, systematising this approach, and teaching it to others. This, after all, is how IADC therapy was truly born.

It was through the combination of Dr Botkin's amazing book and podcast interviews, then watching *Life With Ghosts,* that my path and purpose came to a crescendo. In rapid-fire succession I arranged Zoom calls with the charismatic and ever-curious *Life With Ghosts* filmmaker Stephen Berkley who encouraged me and offered his support, and also Professor Jan Holden and Dr Noelle St. Germain-Sehr, whose study featured in the film. Stephen had devoted seven years to making *Life with Ghosts* and now it was bringing IADC therapy out into the public consciousness, revealing an option for grief that most people would have previously been unaware of. And Professor Holden's study was groundbreaking, with a potentially immense legacy. By comparing IADC therapy with traditional grief counselling, her study was an opportunity to provide scientific and clinical validation to the anecdotal data of Dr Botkin's work to date. Although her study had been completed several years earlier, the resulting scientific paper was 'in press' with a grief journal, but not yet published. To get widespread recognition as an effective therapy, Professor Holden's impressive results[18] would need to be replicated and built upon. I was inspired!

I had an idea to conduct a wait-list controlled trial of IADC therapy in which clients would provide baseline data over a month, would undergo their two ninety-minute sessions, and then I would assess their grief symptoms again a month later. If IADC therapy has the potential to change the way the world deals with grief (as I suspected it did), it could be subjected to rigorous scientific evaluation and the results would be there in black and white for everyone to see. It was time for me to contribute. I launched an IADC research study of my own.

Chapter 16

Carolyn

Carolyn's daughter Phoebe didn't mean to die when she took a handful of Carolyn's heart medication. "It was accidental poisoning," Carolyn told me over our Zoom call. "The coroner wrote: 'This is death by misadventure.' She deliberately took the overdose, but she didn't mean to die."

Carolyn's red hair framed kind eyes as she dialled in to our call from what I surmised was her sewing room. In the background was a stack of random boxes, rolls of fabric, a Himalayan rock salt lamp, and a variety of other odds and ends. Perhaps she has Irish heritage, I thought.

Phoebe was a seventeen-year-old "drama queen" with a strong personality. She was bright, bubbly, and very dramatic, with dreams of becoming an actress or a singer. Her family loved her deeply.

"She was very kind and inclusive. You know, when she played basketball, if we got to a match and the other team didn't have enough players, she'd say, 'Oh, well, let's forget the competition today. We'll just add a few people from our team onto their team so that we can have a good game of basketball.'"

When Phoebe was little, she and Carolyn had a wonderful relationship. Phoebe's early years consisted of playing, laughter, fun, and affection. But when Phoebe hit her teenage years, things became more challenging. "About two years before she died, somebody at her school suicided. Then we had a note from the school that every child had to be taken off for counselling because of this suicide. And then there was this spate of the other kids... a lot of them were self-harming in response to this episode of this child dying by suicide."

Carolyn and her husband went through a challenging time with Phoebe not wanting to go to school, switching schools, and then dropping out altogether. Eventually she seemed to find her feet with babysitting work, and then a job at a local take-away shop. The night before she died, Phoebe had seemed happy when she came home from work.

"She walked in the door, and we said, 'How was your shift? How was your evening?' She said, 'Oh, it was really good.' She said she'd had an argument with a boy at work, but she said, 'The boss took my side, so it was all good.'

"She went off to heat up some Chinese food. We used to live in New York, and in New York, you always ate Chinese food out of a carton. Whereas here, you know, it always comes in plastic boxes. Well, I found a craft shop where they have these boxes, so I bought her some of those. So there she was, eating Chinese with chopsticks out of a carton. And she seemed really happy. And she said, 'Right, I'm going downstairs, good night.' I remember turning to my husband on the couch and saying, 'I think we're over the worst. I think we're over the biggest hump with her, which is really good.'"

Unbeknownst to Carolyn, Phoebe had just watched an episode of *One Tree Hill* that seemed to have set off an idea in her mind.

"The episode that she was watching was where this boy breaks up with the girl. The girl tries to kill herself. The girl gets rescued and goes into hospital, where everybody brings her flowers and chocolates. And then the boy realises that actually he does love her, and they get back together. Well, that's what had happened at the pizza place that night. She'd told this boy that she had a crush on him, which must have taken a lot of guts to do, because I wouldn't do that at that age. He'd told her he wasn't interested."

The next morning, when Phoebe wasn't up by 10 a.m., Carolyn went to wake her, only to find her barely responsive in the bed. As a trained nurse, Carolyn instantly knew something was horribly wrong. Despite more than two hours of attempts to restart her heart, the paramedics and hospital emergency team were unable to revive her.

"I'm a nurse – a mental health nurse, and emergency nurse – I had told my children when they were fairly young that Panadol is a very dangerous drug when you take too much, and you must never overdose on Panadol. You must only ever take the amount that you should. So she didn't touch the Panadol. There was plenty of Panadol in that jar, but she didn't touch it. The reason she died was that I take drugs for my heart which stop it from beating too fast.

"There are two types of drugs. I was weaning off one to start the other. So, I had almost a full packet of the one I was weaning off, and I had the full packet of the one I was about to start with. You cannot take these two drugs together because they will stop the heart. She didn't know that. I never thought to explain that about my drugs. Why would I need to explain it to her?"

There was a look of bewilderment in Carolyn's eyes. I asked her which part of her story brought up the most sadness. I needed to identify the strongest sadness and have her step right into it.

"To let her go," Carolyn said, crying softly. "Not being able to hold on to her. I wanted to just hug her and hug her and just keep hugging her forever.... and I guess hug her back to life."

I got ready to start the bilateral stimulation with eye movement. "I just want you to let yourself feel that, Carolyn," I encouraged her. "I just want you to follow the blue ball, okay?" After the set was done,

I had Carolyn close her eyes for a few seconds, before checking in. "What did you notice happening to your sadness then?" I asked.

"It lessened," she said through tears. "It's still there, but not the intensity."

The eye movement was working straight away. For some clients, their sadness will initially increase – sometimes dramatically – before it comes down again. For others, their sadness decreases from the very first set. Either way, we need to keep processing each piece of sadness until it goes way down. "I want us just to continue and do another set on that same piece of sadness – that you just didn't want to let her go, okay? Just let yourself feel that," I instructed. "You didn't want to let her go... Just follow the blue ball."

We moved quickly. Carolyn was feeling the full depth of her sadness, and I wanted to keep the momentum up. Sometimes it's easy to get sidetracked in thoughts and thinking – analysing and shifting perspectives – and ending up in a traditional counselling role. It would be easy to get sidetracked with a client like Carolyn because she was interesting, she was interested in the therapeutic process, and she was quite psychologically minded. But I needed to avoid that at all costs. The bilateral stimulation would do the work. We just had to stay focused and keep going.

As we progressed, we uncovered Carolyn's sadness at the unfinished story of her daughter's life. A vibrant, talented, and loving girl with so much ahead of her. We stepped in to her devastation at not being able to be a grandmother to Phoebe's future children, to maybe offer Phoebe her own wedding dress. "My son looks like my husband, whereas my daughter looks like me. So, there won't be a grandchild that looks like her. I miss what I don't have, with her not being here."

"Let's do another set on that piece of sadness," I said. "That future that you're missing out on... that she would have been a great mum, and your grandkids would have looked like her and you."

Towards the end of our first session, Carolyn's intense sadness was defined simply: "I just want her back." We did several sets on this, and the sadness began to dissipate, with other feelings coming in. "It's a feeling of acceptance," she told me. "It's not happiness, but it's not sadness. Some acceptance."

Then, happy memories began to bubble up. "Sometimes she'd write me notes and leave them in places, like 'I love you, mum', 'You're the best mum in the world'".

"Let's just do a set on that. Missing her notes, missing what she'd do, how she'd be with you. Let yourself feel that. Follow the blue ball." I administered more eye movement, then asked what she noticed with her sadness that time.

"That's hard to describe. Instead of being sort of, you know, out there, it just sort of feels like it's come in... just inside of me. And I can hold her there. I can hold her inside me. I've never felt that before. It's like, no, I really can hold her inside me. Yeah. I still feel sad, but good. It feels good because it's no longer... that I can't reach her. I *can* reach her."

Carolyn's sadness was changing in a significant way, but this wasn't the time to stop. Bilateral stimulation can rapidly decrease sadness, and you might think that's the point where we'd stop. But in IADC therapy, we expand the good feelings that emerge. I sensed that Carolyn was starting to reconnect with Phoebe in a way she hadn't been able to since Phoebe died.

"I feel kind of more whole. And I can't quite put the words to those feelings. But yeah, it's... sort of a sensation of being whole. You know, she came from me. She was born and she was part of me. Then she was separate and she was external. And she's no longer that external person anymore. It's like she's back inside me. I don't know. It's just... she's there. She's part of me again."

Like NDE testimony, some insights and feelings in IADC, and in particular ADCs themselves, have an ineffable quality. They defy our everyday experience, so it's hard to put into words. By the end of day one I wanted to see many pieces of sadness processed, a reduction in overall state sadness (how the client feels right now), and ideally, some good feelings coming in. Mission accomplished!

The next day we were able to identify two other major pieces of sadness: when the hearse drove away with the coffin, and releasing balloons at Phoebe's wake.

"From the driveway of the funeral home, the hearse goes really slowly. They walk up to the road with this man in front, you know, like the olden days. But as it was leaving, I just remember standing there not wanting it to go. I wanted to say, 'Stop, no, don't go!' I just wanted it to stop. I wanted to run after it. I wanted to just take the coffin out and… I don't know, take it with me or something."

Carolyn initially didn't feel much sadness coming up when we started processing. Sometimes when a lot of sadness is processed on day one it feels harder to get in touch with the sadness at the start of day two. We moved on to the image of the balloons being released, and one stubborn balloon that wouldn't leave.

"Put yourself back there as much as you can," I encouraged her. "And there was that one balloon that wasn't going to go… So just let yourself feel that and follow the blue ball."

Good feelings started to come in. "I just felt love. And then as it went on, all I could do was focus on the blue ball. Yeah. Just this sense of love for her. I guess it's peace. It's just like… it's not strong."

I was now looking for the good feelings to get stronger with each successive set, but the following sets of eye movements didn't progress the feeling very much. I mentally went through the possible reasons why: Carolyn could be intellectualising, thinking too much instead of staying in her emotional brain, but I didn't sense that this was happening for her right now; she could be avoiding her emotions, but this was unlikely as we had arrived at good feelings; or we could simply have arrived at stuck processing, which can occur in EMDR and IADC. This is when – for whatever reason – progress in processing seems to plateau. I suspected the latter. Changing the method of bilateral stimulation was a possible solution for this, so I asked Carolyn to switch to tapping her legs alternately, with her eyes closed. Sometimes switching the method of bilateral stimulation can help get things back on track if processing seems stuck. I wanted to keep Carolyn relaxed, to have her go with the flow, and not get caught up in judging what was happening or analysing the process in any way.

It worked.

"I couldn't think of any of the sad images that time. All I was thinking of was the fun ones, which I haven't thought about in so long. And just funny things that she said and did. There was this time we were at a music camp, she must have been seven, I think. She must have had a discussion with the orchestra leader beforehand, because at the end of the camp, we'd given the prizes, we were doing the final concert, and the orchestra leader said, 'Phoebe's got something to say'. And Phoebe walked up onto the stage with the present in her hand, just all of seven years old, and says 'I want to thank my mum. She's done a great job here, along with all the teachers, but she's been here and she's helped some people, and she's a really good mum!' She came and gave me a present. And I mean, it was just gorgeous; so sweet."

Pleasant memories were a good sign, but I didn't direct Carolyn to go back to specific memories. It was more important she stay with the feeling, in the present moment, and see what unfolds next. IADC is an emotion-driven therapy, and the rule is, if emotions are changing, it's working. Further sets of tapping helped these good feelings to grow, and I watched in amazement as I always do with this therapy, as her healing occurred in just two ninety-minute sessions.

"I feel warm. It's sort of like I want her to be here, and I wish I could feel her more tangibly. But I think... well, this warmth that I'm feeling is kind of... it's like she's inside me. You know, she's part of me. She's here. It's almost like she was wrapping her arms around me, but not quite that tangible."

I wanted to understand from Carolyn's point of view what kind of shift was occurring for her, as this sense of reconnection with her daughter emerged. "What does it mean to you that now you have this sense of reconnection... that she's inside you, and it feels good?" I asked.

"Well, it means a kind of sense of freedom. Yeah, I can just get on with things now. It's like... okay, I expect there will be moments of sadness at some point in the future, which will just be when you think about something. But there's not that sense of loss so much anymore. And it's just like.... okay. She's still there, she's still part of my life, just in a very different way. And it's just coming and going. It'll be a bit like life would be anyway. If she'd gone on and got married, I wouldn't be seeing her every day. You come in and go out, and you get on with your own things. You don't ever stop being a mother, but your children do move away. But they're still there in your thoughts. Well, it's just like that. Yeah... it's like the loss has gone. I am connected with her."

One way of verifying progress is to see if previously distressing images have changed, so I asked Carolyn, "When you now cast your mind to those memories that you'd said were distressing at the start today – like the coffin being driven away – how do you feel now when you think about that?".

"I don't see it very well. I mean, it's there, but it's been replaced. Instead of seeing it driving away, I see the hearse with the coffin in it, but I'm standing there hugging my husband instead." When images become harder to see or recall, or they change, it corresponds with a decrease in distress. Some theories suggest bilateral stimulation causes a 'rewiring' of the neuronal pathways; different networks of the brain are then activated after the therapy. This idea is consistent with what we see clinically in cases such as Carolyn.

"It doesn't matter that the car will drive away because she's still here. That's the big thing. The big thing is I don't have that sense of loss. I don't need to yearn for her or miss her, because I still have her."

Carolyn didn't have an elaborate after-death communication in her therapy sessions with me, but what she gained was more important: a renewed sense of connection to her daughter, and a healing of the deep sense of loss that she'd been carrying for years. Healing Carolyn's grief wasn't going to bring her daughter back, but it would enable her to live her life without the weight of sadness.

Chapter 17

Karma is Now

I have consumed hundreds, perhaps thousands of cases of NDEs, ADCs, and all kinds of spiritual phenomena through books, scientific papers, documentaries, videos, and podcasts. The most consistent and compelling feature of any of these stories is the life review reported by those who have near-death experiences. Variously described as panoramic, holographic, or even featuring screens, the life review isn't merely visual. It provides the ability to feel the emotions of each person we interact with in our life, the effects of our actions, and how they reflect our personality, love, and spiritual evolution. Some of the life reviews have stuck with me and influenced the way I now live my life. More than any other spiritual phenomenon, I believe the life review teaches us the most about how to live on this side of the veil.

One such NDE testimony that moved me was that of medical student George Ritchie[31]. At just 20 years of age in 1943, and stationed in Fort Berkeley, Texas at the height of World War II, he was struck down with severe pneumonia and a fever of 106.5F (41C) that lasted for days. Ritchie was eventually pronounced dead and had the bed sheets drawn up over his head. Despite his seemingly lifeless body lying there waiting to be taken to the morgue, Ritchie was awake and aware, outside of his body. He found himself flying above a town that he had never before visited, which he later learned was Vicksburg, Mississippi.

On realising he needed to get back to the army base in order to catch a train home in time for Christmas, he found himself walking the rows of army cots in the base hospital. The only feature that allowed him to identify himself among the row of bodies was the cygnet ring on his left hand, dangling off the side of the bed. As he pondered how to get back into that seemingly lifeless body and reanimate it somehow, he saw a blindingly bright light emerge from one side of the room. A booming voice pronounced: "Stand up, for you are in the presence of the Son of God." Humbled by the presence of Jesus, a life review commenced.

Ritchie explained: "I have never been in the presence of such total and absolute love, a Being that totally knew everything about me and totally accepted me and totally loved me. A moment before, desperately alone and frightened, awful gloom. Now to be in the presence of this Being, I didn't want to leave Him under any circumstance. This Christ is like something you have never seen. I don't have the words to get this across."

"What did you do with your life?" Jesus asked.

Ritchie writes: "It seemed to be question about values, not facts: What did you accomplish with the precious time you were allotted?" Aware that communication in this dimension was telepathic, and therefore his mind could be read, he was perturbed. "Desperately I looked around me for something that would seem worthwhile in the light of this blazing Reality. It wasn't that there were spectacular sins, just the sexual hang-ups and secretiveness of most teenagers. But if there were no horrendous depths, there were no heights either. Only an endless, shortsighted, clamorous concern for myself."

He began to think of all the impressive things he could proclaim in answer: being an eagle scout; president of his college fraternity. It didn't seem to impress Jesus much. In his desperate and clumsy attempts to justify his worth in Jesus' presence, he realised Jesus was laughing. Not in a mocking way, but a joyful, paternal, loving laughter. It eventually dawned on young Ritchie that "He was not asking about accomplishments and awards. The question, like everything else proceeding from Him, had to do with love. How much have you loved with your life? Have you loved others as I am loving you? Totally? Unconditionally?"

The night shift orderly thought he saw Ritchie move, after nine minutes had passed without a heartbeat. His return was the beginning of a life inspired by the lessons of his life review, and the presence of a spiritual force so loving and powerful it informed everything he did.

I pondered my answer to the question "What have you done with your life?" What would I say? How would Jesus react to my answer? Had I loved with my life? I'd certainly been on the receiving end of a loving life. Nanna loved me totally, unconditionally, and she devoted herself to the care of others. Her quiet, unassuming life would have pleased Jesus, I'm sure.

Another near-death experiencer whose post-NDE life was inspired by his anticipation of his next life review was Dannion Brinkley, who you will recall from earlier in this book is a multiple NDE survivor. He explained how his experience of reviewing his life out of body, fundamentally changed the way he lives his life. Speaking at Chicago IANDS in 2005, he related one incident from one of his multiple life reviews in which he defended five homeless women who were being accosted by a gang of thugs[9].

"I looked down the street corner there was five women with shopping carts, and this gang of six guys, and they all backed up together holding their shopping carts. And these guys were picking at them and trying to turn their carts over and all this stuff. Well, I picked me up a little two by four... and I worked that crowd over good. Because when you're not afraid, and they think they're gonna frighten you, you have the upper edge. And I beat 'em good... I beat 'em really good... four of them I hurt pretty bad."

On the face of it, his violent act might seem to be the kind of thing that would be disapproved of in the afterlife. But Brinkley revealed the crucial part of the life review is not just your actions in any moment, but the *intent* behind it. "I took those ladies into a Chinese restaurant and... covered for them so they could go in the bathroom and wash and shower and eat. We sat at the buffet – we stayed there for five hours. And I was enjoying it because I was watching girls talk, you know? And they were safe, you know? And they've been living on the street for years." His subsequent life review allowed him to see the effects of his actions. "I got to be them looking in the mirror in the bathroom washing their hair, cleaning up, and being able to see and feel that joy."

He beat off the thugs with violence but what shone through in his life review was his intention, because when you have your life review, "you're going to know the reason why you did what you did... You could have just hurt their feelings because you were mad – well, you're going to feel that anger. You're going to feel that hurt. Or, you could've said something to them that made them angry, but it was you trying to help them, and you care about them, and you appreciate them... Always remember, it's never what, it's *why*."

I examined the intent behind my life decisions and found I didn't have an easy answer to the question 'why?' Why did I work as a psychologist? Why was I doing IADC research? Often there was more than one reason. I need to work to pay the bills, but I also want to help others. I'm doing my IADC research because I feel compelled to help bring this therapy to the world. My conclusion from Dannion Brinkley and George Ritchie's stories was that if I maintained a loving intent as much as possible, in as many decisions as possible, I'd better my chances of having a pleasant life review. I would have lived according to this higher spiritual purpose: loving with your life. If this is what Jesus, God, or the Universe wants from us, it can be taken as a measure and means to spiritual evolution.

Karen Thomas' life review unveiled the far-reaching consequences of her every action and thought, even beyond the emotions of the person immediately influenced by her[32]. She recounts: "It was really amazing to see how wonderful some things were, in terms of maybe a small kindness that I thought I had done. It was so positive for the other individual that they went on and did more positive things; I saw this huge ripple effect of how much impact your behaviour and your thoughts and actions literally have on other people.

"I felt bad for ones where I wasn't acting very well to somebody else, and they were hurt, and then they felt badly and did something badly to someone else… I felt bad about those things, but I didn't feel any sort of judgment." Karen's experience reminds us of the interconnectedness of our lives and the ripple effect of our choices. Every interaction, no matter how seemingly insignificant, has the potential to shape the lives of others.

The more I consumed NDE cases, one theme became clear: it isn't the high-stakes moments when we're weighing the consequences of something big that constitutes the spiritual success of our lives. Every single interaction is important. Every moment, thought, and intent reflects the content of our spiritual character and leaves an imprint in the universe, forever. This indelible imprint is the true legacy of a life well lived. Not just the big, dramatic moments, but all the little ones we think are insignificant. *Especially* the little ones.

The story of John J Davis suggested to me that even when you think nobody's watching, somebody or something is. He ended up in hospital after crashing his scooter into a tree. As a healthy 21-year-old, he'd never before had reason to have an operation, but his hand was so badly damaged in the accident, he needed to have it surgically repaired. But John's lack of major surgeries meant he – and his doctors – didn't know he was allergic to a common anaesthetic, and his body went into major shock. He found himself out of his body and was provided with a guided tour of the afterlife by a benevolent spirit guide. In one particularly striking moment, John was taken to a large round room with screens for his life review[33]:

"...all of a sudden, the screens lit up. Like they were playing movies... like I was in the theatre. In every screen that I could see had a different aspect of my life. One was playing when I was just a newborn. Another one was playing when I was an infant. Another one was playing when I started elementary school, and then went all the way through these. Every screen had a different aspect of my life up to the age that I was then, age 21." John realised that every moment of our lives is recorded, a concept he attributes to the divine: "...everything is recorded... this has to be a God thing. I cannot comprehend how it's possible that everything is recorded. But it is. That's why when we have our life reviews, you're able to see everything about your life. It's somehow in God's mind. It's recorded."

At first this was daunting to me, conjuring images of a cosmic surveillance system designed to catch us in our missteps. But then I realised it's the only truly fair and accurate system of self-evaluation there is. No self-serving bias, nothing hidden. Just our spiritual nakedness in full view – who we truly are. This realisation invites us to live differently, to try to grasp that our every action and interaction is indelibly imprinted on the fabric of existence. Social psychologists have long observed that humans behave differently when they know they are being watched, even by a single person. Imagine, then, the profound shift that could occur if we lived with the acute awareness that not only are our actions recorded, but that we will one day re-live them from the perspectives of those we influenced – for better or worse. And not only that, we'll immediately see the intention behind each action (the *why*), and the ripple effect that goes out beyond the immediate circumstance.

The life review as described by John Davis and countless other experiencers is not a forum of external judgment or punishment, it's a catalyst for self-reflection and growth. It offers us a chance to assess our lives with perfect clarity, to celebrate the moments we fulfilled our soul's mission, and to learn from the times we fell short.

Another realisation that changed the way I evaluated my life, was about what constitutes 'success' from a spiritual viewpoint. Much like George Ritchie, Chrystal Rae was surprised as to what was highlighted as her most positive achievements. While her vehicle careened off an 80-foot cliff, Chrystal watched from above in the presence of a divine being of light. In her life review, Chrystal was lovingly shown the ripple effects of her actions[34]: "I was shown my every good and bad deed, thought, and action, and there was absolutely no judgment but the judgment that I brought upon myself. To the contrary, I mean, truthfully, there was just a lot of compassion for me for any judgment or shame or guilt that I might have about my actions."

Even more surprising than the lack of judgement, Chrystal found that 'success' as it is typically defined was of little value in the afterlife.

"Success in a career, or economic financial success, or success as in getting accolades like an award or a plaque on the wall, or diploma, or even being famous or any of the things that we might consider to be success in our terms, was not what I was shown as my success. What I was shown was random acts of kindness where I actually cared for another, did a benevolent act with no need of reciprocation, just wanting to help another from the goodness of my heart."

How often did I truly act from the goodness of my heart? I tried to recall instances of helping someone without any expectation of something in return. I was concerned at how long it took me to think of examples.

If our intentions are laid bare for the universe, God, *somebody*, to see and know, does this include our private thoughts? In her interview on the *Grief 2 Growth* podcast with Brian D. Smith, near-death experiencer Penny Whitbrodt shared some powerful insights she gained during her experience about the very real effects our thoughts can have[35]:

"God showed me, he said, 'Let me explain something to you. So, a thought has a certain measure of energy to it, and a word has even more, and an action has more than that, but it all starts with a thought.' When you have a negative thought about that person, that energy goes out there, and it attaches itself to that person… you contribute to the jerk that that person is because now you've attached more of that energy to them. So this is why forgiving is so important."

After hearing Penny Whitbrodt's amazing story I found myself becoming instantly aware when judgemental thoughts entered my consciousness. I could catch them, revoke them, and even mentally send encouragement, love, and goodwill to that person. If my intention and thoughts mattered, and if energy is broadcast by us in a way that manifests and affects others, I wanted to change what I was sending out through my usual mental commentary that contained far more judgements than I'd care to admit.

The inevitable life review implores us to infuse our daily lives with greater meaning and purpose. Each interaction becomes an opportunity to create a life review we can one day experience with joy and satisfaction. But if death happens to be a long way away, how do we remind ourselves to live each day inspired by this reality? It was presumptuous of me to assume my life review was a long way away – but I did anyway – and it made me feel less accountable. Karmic procrastination. Yet I had come to believe that our impact on others is the measure of our life, our intention matters, and – as strange as it sounds – everything is recorded. I needed to create a good answer to the question 'What have you done with your life?' If I was going to apply these spiritual insights and really live the way I suspected I should, I needed something to help me evaluate my life and progress much sooner than my death... like, today.

The Day Review

Worried that I'd forget to apply these principles until it was too late, I started doing something I call the Day Review. It's a daily reflection, whereby I recall each major interaction with others, imagining how it was experienced by the other person. This one daily practice has completely changed my life by bringing a depth of thoughtfulness, empathy, and self-control I didn't realise I had. You can do it too.

Your day review will only take 5 minutes (or less) and is a small investment in your spiritual life. But the return on investment will be extraordinary. Here's how to do it:

Step 1. Pick a regular time in your routine when you have absolute quiet and will be uninterrupted. I like to do this in bed, immediately before I go to sleep. But you could choose any quiet location or time at the end of the day that suits you.

Step 2. Replay the day back in your mind, from the moment you get up to the moment you do the review. You don't have to go through every single thing, of course, but all the main things you do, paying particular attention to your interactions with others. For example, interactions with your spouse, your child, the checkout operator at the supermarket, and anyone you speak to on the phone.

Step 3. Reflect on how others experienced your influence. How did your presence in their life make them feel? Did it help them? Even if your interaction with someone involved you or them experiencing negative emotions, what was the intent behind the interaction? Was it coming from a place of love and kindness (even tough love) or was it selfish, impulsive, or shortsighted?

This process allows you to gauge how that day's actions will likely be seen from the spiritual point of view. Oh, and it's not just what we do, it's what we don't do. The time not taken, the phone call left unreturned. All these have consequences that go beyond what we could ever see or measure in our ordinary lives. Remember: the most ordinary of interactions matter for our spiritual lives.

I believe the Day Review is the most truly spiritual practice you can possibly do. Being fully aware of the ramifications of your life, every day, examining your mark on the world. Your ripple. The things that people think and feel when you interact with them. Sure, it is an imagined sense of what they think and feel, but here your intuition will guide you. You'll recall your intent in each moment. Surprising things will stand out – the tone in your voice, a fleeting shift in the other person's expression or body language – inviting you to pause and reflect further. Sometimes, unhappy at how I'd handled something, or ashamed at my performance, I would send a prayer after that person. I'd make a mental note of something I would do the next day to correct it, or simply resolve to behave differently next time. It took lots of self-compassion to not simply remonstrate with myself and feel regretful. Over time, it inspired me to do better, to remember my intent, and filled me with a serene warmth when I noticed more good, unselfish acts.

I was changing. In a funny sort of way, I was becoming more spiritual. Not as in meditating or attempting astral travel, but in conducting myself in the ordinary context of my daily life as the kind of spiritual being I now know myself to be.

Be warned: once you start this there's no going back. You can't unsee your influence rolling out in real time. It'll change your thoughts, too. Instead of bouncing around like a pinball on autopilot, you'll become more conscious, deliberate. Initially, I was shocked at the sheer volume of judgemental thoughts I had.

Doesn't she know lip filler never makes anyone look better?

Could this guy scan his groceries any slower?

Stevie Wonder could drive better than this old granny!

But I would now catch those thoughts. I could reflect, rewind, and change my attitude and intent. In time, it changed the way I thought about and interacted with others, for the better. It made me a better person. It'll make you a better person too.

Eventually, something magical will happen. You'll start thinking about your day review *during the day*. Eventually, you'll have a sublime sensitivity to each moment while you're interacting with others. The depth with which you perceive life will magnify, and you'll start to notice things that would have otherwise been lost to your awareness. Time will slow down. You will notice forks in the road, choices to do or not do something *with the other person in mind*. You will even find yourself – momentarily – as a proxy for God. Because you will notice opportunities to be the answer to someone's prayers. You will find yourself in the right place at the right time. In small but oh-so-important ways, you'll be the shining light and love of the universe.

Chapter 18

Bethany

Bethany arrived at my consulting room having flown from interstate to be part of my University of Adelaide IADC therapy trial. She looked significantly younger than her 50-odd years and had a warm, friendly presence that belied the intense sadness lurking underneath. With curly, sandy-blonde hair and a sun-kissed look, she was reminiscent of a surfer girl. I imagined her spending time outdoors in the sun, at the beach.

Bethany was a young mum, only twenty years old, when she had her first son, Sean. Her love for Sean, and her sadness since his death, was the reason she had asked to participate in this relatively obscure, and very brief, form of grief therapy. Over two days she would see me for a total of three hours, in which I would attempt to reduce the sadness that was so affecting her life, four years since Sean's passing. She had flown a long way at significant cost to try to find relief. I admired her courage and determination.

As she settled in the high-backed leather chair, with the tissue box strategically placed within reach and a bottle of water nearby, I asked Bethany to tell me about Sean's personality.

"The first word that comes to mind is 'big'. Funny. Like smart and witty. His emotional intelligence for a young man was beyond his years. He was always curious about everybody and the world. And he definitely had a bit of a wicked side."

When Sean reached adulthood, she noticed their relationship changed to one of more equals, with a deep friendship. "He and I just totally got each other. Even when we were arguing – we never had big arguments – but we'd have discussions on topical issues or, you know, if he'd been a bit slack – because he could be a bit slack about things. Even when we were having these interactions, it was like kind of ribbing each other. There was an element of joy in even our arguments."

Sean and Bethany would talk on the phone for hours. As she described their relationship, she was able to identify one of her strongest pieces of sadness. "I can't talk to anybody about things like I could talk to him, because he just had the same curiosity as me. I loved that about him."

The day Sean died, he was on cloud nine. He had just signed on six new clients for a fledgling business venture. He wanted to 'step up' for his new girlfriend and start planning a life together. It finally felt like everything was falling into place for him.

"I've never heard him so happy. I remember thinking to myself, 'My God, you sound so happy you could burst.'" Sean's partner was on the last day of her law degree. "It was like the whole world was about to open up for them."

Sean told Bethany about his plans for the rest of the day: he'd go for a swim, wait for his younger brother to come home, then they'd have a 'jam' playing music together. "I said, 'that sounds really good'. And so evidently what he did is, he went down to the pool, and he was doing that stupid fucking breathing exercise that they do along with cold exposure. Everyone's like, 'it's the best'. Have you ever heard of it? Yeah. It sucks. They don't explain to people what it actually does, which is make them hypoxic."

Bethany was clearly sad, but she was angry too. Angry at the senseless nature of her son's death. She leant forward, waving her arms as she spoke.

"And then on the videos, they show all these young men, like, oh, not only is this great… like, you get a high… but look how long you can hold your breath in icy water for. So Sean had gone and done the exercises, then jumped in the water, and laid on the bottom of the pool to see how long he could hold his breath for. But he was hypoxic. And of course, I now know that you shouldn't do that when you're hypoxic, because your body does not know to come up. But they don't tell people!"

The intensity in Bethany's eyes, the sharp tone in her voice, commanded attention. The sheer injustice of her son's preventable death added a cutting edge to her sorrow.

"His brother Daniel came home, and couldn't find Sean," she paused. "Daniel had seen Sean the afternoon before, laying on the bottom of the pool doing this meditation, and he had come up that time. But this time, he didn't come up. He was just laying at the bottom of the pool, and my 18-year-old son had to pull him out.

"Daniel must have known at that point that Sean was gone, because he'd been there for a couple of hours," Bethany sniffled through tears. "And he had to call me and tell me. You know, tried to revive him, and, yeah… it was pretty awful for him."

By now, Bethany was really accessing her sadness. I wanted to get into the processing as quickly as possible and start working through what I could tell was going to be a huge amount of sadness.

"When you think about everything you've talked about, this incredible connection that you've had with Sean, his wonderful personality, his life and all those good qualities, *and* the circumstances of his death, and everything since then… what is it that brings up the most sadness for you right now?" I asked.

"I mean, it's obviously that I'm missing him," she said, her eyes searching, feeling for the sadness. "His physical presence, and having someone that kind of gets me, you know? And then, because we are a little bit quirky, I didn't realize how much that just having that one person made it easier to tolerate everything else in life. I didn't realise that – I don't know if it's dysfunctional or whatever – but there were things that I got from my relationship with my son that I didn't need to get from my partner. And now, all of a sudden, it's not there, and it just makes me feel so alone."

So alone.

When I heard those words, I felt a pang in my stomach. Yet again, I was on the precipice of crying, getting caught up in my client's story of loss. Even though I was trying to be present for Bethany, somewhere in the recesses of my mind there was the ache of imagining what it would be like to lose my son. I had to shake it off and stay focused. It was time to start the bilateral stimulation.

I had Bethany place her hands on her knees as I moved my office chair in closer so I could tap the back of her hands alternately. With her eyes closed, I wanted Bethany to let herself be washed away into the full depth of her feelings, with just the metronomic rhythm of my gentle tapping punctuating her awareness. We could have used eye movements, with Bethany following my raised finger in the air moving back and forth horizontally like a metronome. Either one would work, but today we started with tapping.

"I just want you to let yourself feel that missing him feeling… Just let yourself feel that, and let the feelings come up, okay?" I spoke softly as I leant in and started the rhythmic tapping.

After the first set I asked Bethany what happened to her sadness.

"I started talking to myself, actually," she said.

I ignored Bethany's thinking, as I had been trained to do, and instead focused on the sadness. "Did the sadness increase or decrease?"

"It decreased. It's really interesting how my mind goes into soothing myself and talking to myself," she said.

I didn't want her to talk to herself, but I also didn't want to further add to her mental regulation strategies by telling her *not* to think. In psychology there's a thing called Ironic Process Theory: it's when you try not to think of something, there's a rebound effect and you think about it more. I'd co-authored a research paper in which we tested the theory by having people try to block out intrusive thoughts. Trying to block out thoughts didn't work.

"Just try to let the mental chatter sit at the side," I encouraged.

The next few sets brought forth more tears.

"What did you notice that time?" I asked after another set of tapping.

"It's really interesting because I actually started thinking again. Then I went, 'No, I just want to feel it'. And I felt it in my chest – the sadness sat there – and then I felt it move down into my belly, and then I felt new grief. I literally tracked it. That was interesting. I tried not to get too angry at him."

"Angry at him for what happened?" I asked.

"Yeah. Because I knew that he'd be kicking himself more than anyone else. He didn't like making mistakes."

As Dr Allan Botkin wrote about in his book *Induced After Death Communication*, anger is a masking emotion, just like guilt. It's easier, less painful, or more energising to feel anger than it is to feel sad. This is why we always direct the client back to the sadness – even badger them if we have to – because sadness is at the core of grief. That's why Dr Botkin originally called his approach Core-Focused EMDR. It ignored the peripheral emotions to go straight to the core: sadness. The dissolving of which automatically results in the dissolving of anger and guilt. I needed to direct Bethany back to her sadness.

"Is it the case that the anger, if we really look behind that anger…I'm guessing there's also sadness," I said.

"Of course," she agreed.

"Let's go for the sadness," I said. "Let yourself feel the sadness behind the anger."

During the next set, Bethany reported feeling dizzy. Then, that her ears were about to pop. And she could also feel the emotion in her belly. This is known as the 'somatisation' of a client's emotions and is quite common. They don't just feel their emotions, they feel it in their body as well. This wasn't necessarily a problem, rather it was something to keep track of. The bodily tension goes hand in hand with the emotion, and if the processing of the emotion gets stuck, we can try focusing directly on the bodily sensation while applying bilateral stimulation. Amongst all the tears and crying and nose blowing, Bethany was courageously confronting her most intense feelings. My job was to keep her going, to not let her get distracted, and to keep her foot on the gas. Even when it gets intense, we mustn't stop. We go *through* the sadness, to get to the peace on the other side.

"My eyes are so puffed. I'm crying so much. I can't breathe," She said. "I think I was just trying to let go of the thoughts. And they were just too intrusive for me to actually feel anything."

We were making some progress. There were some decreases in the sadness and some feelings of peacefulness emerging, but I wanted to move faster. Bethany had flown from interstate to see me in Adelaide, and we didn't have unlimited time. I wanted to push through as much processing as we could so she could go home a different person, just as I'd seen happen for many of my other clients.

"It's like me going into battle with myself in a way," she explained. "I can feel like there's a level of peace, but then my brain switches in. When my thinking clicks in, it kind of unravels it a bit."

I really liked Bethany. We'd built a good rapport. I liked her no-nonsense attitude and her humour. She was interesting to talk to, thoughtful, and was someone who clearly loved and cared deeply about those around her. But she could also be blunt.

"Your water sucks and you need a bigger bin!" she laughed while wiping away more tears.

"I bought a new box of tissues just for you!" I retorted as we laughed.

When we did the next set, she seemed to relax a little more, and had one of those spontaneous realisations I had come to expect from IADC therapy: "It's like somehow I know that he's actually at peace with it. Maybe it's just me that's not, you know? I get a sense that from his perspective, it is what it is. In terms of being sad for the future he missed out on, there's a peace, a sense of peace coming from him... that he's okay."

Bethany was pensive now, just sniffling occasionally. While gazing at the wall, at nothing in particular, she pondered the idea that Sean was at peace. As if she was soaking this new realisation in. Then, she looked back to me and spoke with certainty:

"Well, that's true: he's okay with it. And he's made it really clear."

This was a sign of more progress, but I wanted to keep pushing her forward. The nature of IADC therapy is that it's intense. We relentlessly pursue the reduction of sadness through bilateral stimulation, speeding through the sadness like a Formula One car, where EMDR would meander along. Why so fast? Because once we step into the vulnerable, powerful, active processing we don't want to stop until we get through the pain. We go through the dark tunnel to the light at the other end. We don't want to dawdle and dwell in the painful burn of tragedy and loss, we don't want our clients to sit in that state a moment longer than they need to, and we don't want to give them a chance to go back to their old, incomplete, attempts to manage how they feel. We want to change how they feel about the loss in a big way – and permanently. Who wants to spend twelve weekly sessions on a therapist's couch talking about the worst thing that happened to them, when it can be done in two days?

"So your sadness now is the sadness of what you're missing out on, not having him there in your life?" I asked.

She nodded.

"He would have been the most fabulous father," she implored. "And he always *knew*." Bethany was looking at me intently again now. "Honestly, I need to tell you this… he told everybody that he was going to die at 27."

"Did he?"

"Everybody."

"Really?"

"As a joke. 'I'm going to join the 27 club'."

"And was he 27 when he died?"

"Of course he was. Two weeks short of turning 28. So I think he was always at peace with it. And I just really got the distinct feeling, like… he's okay with it. I literally felt that."

The next piece of sadness that Bethany identified was to do with regrets. But when we finished the set of tapping, she said "I went through my mental list of things I regretted." She was getting caught up in thoughts again, mentally trying to control the processing rather than simply allowing the bilateral stimulation to do the work. By trying to make mental lists, or creating imagery, rather than being an observer of how her sadness was changing (and anything else that naturally arose), she was inhibiting the processing.

I had noticed that Bethany was very observant, precise in her communication, and somewhat mentally controlled. I needed her to relax into the flow of the sets of tapping or eye movement. To not worry about ugly crying, or how many tissues were going everywhere, or trying to analyse what was happening. By using her thoughts to direct the processing, rather than just step into the sadness as I had instructed, Bethany was both holding herself back from feeling the full intensity of her emotional pain and putting the brakes on the therapy working.

She was blocking it for a reason, and I can't say I blame her. Blocking the distressing sadness of having lost her eldest son in such a needless way was a strategy she would have required at times to simply function. Work, friendships, and life in general can't easily accommodate someone in deep emotional pain. Avoidance, suppression, and regulation are essential tools that allow a grieving mother to simply keep going. And it can't be easy to dive headlong into the full burn of the worst thing that has ever happened to you, with a perfect stranger (me) relentlessly taking her back into the worst aspects of that experience.

We finished up that first day with Bethany feeling exhausted. I was concerned that we might run out of time. Perhaps tomorrow she'll be more relaxed, will know what to expect, and we can go hard, I thought. Perhaps eye movement would work better as focusing on my moving fingers would take more mental effort than having her eyes closed with me tapping the back of her hands. She'd have less mental energy for getting caught up in thinking, and could stay with the feeling.

Bethany arrived at my small, rented office on the second day of our IADC therapy sessions eager to tell me about a profound lucid dream she had experienced the night before. "I was at this Helping Parents Heal conference," she began. "And then I find myself walking towards this beach house, and I tripped, and as I tripped, I realised, 'Oh, I'm dreaming'. I just went, 'I'm gonna fly', and I was just wide awake [fully conscious and aware in the dream], flying, going, 'Oh, just take this in. This feels really good.'"

In the experience, Bethany saw a giant figure that she intuitively knew was Sean. When she expanded herself to his size, he came running towards her. "Oh, finally," he said as they embraced. "Finally." They flew together, with Sean telling Bethany "It feels good, doesn't it, Mum?" She described their communication as telepathic, a resonance more than a conversation. Sean reassured her that he liked it where he was, that there was a lot of variety.

I was amazed but not entirely surprised by Bethany's account. Spontaneous ADCs occurring between sessions is a phenomenon I'd witnessed before with this therapy. Her experience that morning showed the enduring strength of her connection with Sean, even though she had been feeling disconnected from him recently as she grappled with other life challenges. Dream or 'sleep' ADCs are among the most commonly reported types of spontaneously occurring ADCs. Unlike my ADCs with my grandparents, Bethany wasn't just being visited, her lucid dream placed her *in* another dimension with Sean. The literature on lucid dreams and out of body experiences includes much debate on whether these are actually variations of the same phenomenon. I'm inclined to believe they are. And the feeling of floating, flying, and interacting with the world separate from your body, yet with full awareness, is possibly as close as we can get to a near-death experience without actually being close to death!

As we began the second day's session, I encouraged Bethany to radically accept her emotions, as difficult as that might be. "It's going to be okay. You've got to trust the process," I told her gently but firmly. The only way out was *through*. "I want us to do a set on letting go of control, letting go of thinking," I said. As Bethany followed my fingers for the eye movements, I watched tears leak out freely from the corner of her eyes. She wasn't fighting it anymore, just courageously confronting her grief head-on. "Let yourself feel it…"

"What did you notice?" I asked, referring to her sadness, after the end of each set.

"Once you're in, it doesn't feel as overwhelming," she reported.

The bilateral stimulation was helping her to process the sadness rather than be consumed by it. Bethany identified the tragic story of her life as a major piece of sadness – the hardships she had endured culminating in the loss of her extraordinary son.

"It's like, how could one life be so unlucky, you know?"

We processed that sadness through many sets of eye movements. "I could literally feel something click," Bethany said, describing a physical sensation of the emotional shift taking place. The realisations from Sean, her lucid dream, and reducing sadness, had all helped Bethany to feel closer to Sean. In the couple of years I had been doing IADC therapy, I had learnt that when the sadness reduces, it reliably gives way to good feelings – something grieving people don't usually expect from a two-session therapy. I felt we were getting close to that shift now. Although it was exhausting, Bethany set aside her impulse to overthink and judge the process. She surrendered to actually feeling her feelings, trusting that it would get her to the other side of the pain.

"The moment thoughts popped up, you just let it pass by, like a train going through a station," I observed. "You're not clinging onto it. We're really just letting the eye movements do the work."

Gradually, as expected, the sadness continued to soften, and peaceful feelings emerged. We did a few sets focused on expanding that peace and calm. "It's like releasing this allows me to step forward more into relaxing," Bethany reflected, breathing deeply.

By the end of our session, she was emotionally spent but feeling better. "I feel very happy," she said with a tired smile, "but not in a bad way." I understood what Bethany meant. It wasn't a simple, uncomplicated happiness, but rather a bittersweet mix of emotions. The happiness came from the relief of finally releasing all the pent-up grief she had been carrying, and from the renewed sense of connection to Sean that had emerged. But there was also an acknowledgment that this didn't fully erase the pain of losing him or the challenges that lay ahead.

"I still feel like I've got shit to work out," she added, with characteristic bluntness. The road forward wouldn't be easy, but she seemed to have a new resilience and clarity to face it head-on.

Although Bethany didn't have an ADC during the session itself, she experienced a phenomenon that sometimes occurs in IADC therapy: when ADC's happen *between* sessions. The dream visitation from Sean that morning seemed to set the stage for the breakthroughs she experienced in processing her grief. She left with a renewed sense of connection to her son and the conviction that she would be okay – two gifts that would fortify her for whatever lay ahead.

The wall of sadness she had been holding back for so long had come down, opening up space for peace, clarity, and hope to emerge. Her love for Sean, and his love for her, remained as strong as ever – that would never change. But Bethany was no longer weighed down by the tragic story of her life. She was free to move forward and live fully again. Sean would be right there with her, cheering her on in spirit, as she did.

I caught up with Bethany over Zoom about seven weeks later to check in and answer any questions she might have as a result of participating in the research project. I asked her how she had been going since our sessions.

"Really good," she said. "This therapy... It's almost like... I felt guilty because I haven't felt the same level of sadness. Is that okay? I had to really think.... Is that okay?"

I smiled. I'd encountered this ambivalence about letting go of sadness in so many of my grieving clients. "You know, that's why I really make a point of asking people every time now: 'Do you think you would be okay if you didn't feel as sad?'"

I explained to Bethany how a previous client had been crying daily, which stopped after her IADC sessions with me. She later told me that although it was surprising and somewhat of a relief to feel less sad, she was also annoyed with me as she now felt she had to move forward in her life.

"I actually understand!" Bethany exclaimed, "I understand why she would think like that!"

I asked Bethany for her feedback on the therapy.

"You know, I had high hopes, but I remained open to the possibilities of how I might actually feel. But I've got to tell you, I am shocked at how effective it is. I just can't believe that I don't feel as sad. It's a strange sensation in a way. It's like the whole thing is still there, but the gravity of the emotion is just... lifted."

Chapter 19

Living an Inspired Life

I f life reviews show us how people feel interacting with us, does that mean we need to be gushing over others, repressing our needs, never making demands, never saying no? If we only need to make others feel good, then what about the parent denying their child? Or the lover ending a relationship that isn't right? Should we always prioritise what'll make the other person simply feel the best in that moment? No. What matters is both our intention and our effect. In other words: were you inspired by love? Not love in a romantic sense, but the love that spurs caring and helping. The love that wishes another being well.

A distressed teenager whose parents have refused her permission to go to the unsupervised party, a heartbroken lover mourning the loss of a partner who recognised the unhealthy dynamic in their relationship, or a young child frustrated and angered by the rules of the house, are all beneficiaries of loving intent. Long-term positive outcomes are often the result of short-term pain. Our influence could be a single interaction, a piece of advice, a moment of compassion… or it could be a lifetime friendship with many ups and downs. It's the intent behind our actions that matters most.

When I soaked in this central theme of life reviews in NDEs – the most robust evidentiary data from the other side – and started doing the Day Review exercise before I went to sleep each night, it changed me. I tried to not be so consumed with selfish thoughts and tried to express love in my actions. I became more patient driving my car. Where before I would wander the aisles of the grocery store consumed with my own wants and needs, I instead tried to remember my loving intent, smiling at strangers and hoping for an opportunity to retrieve an out-of-reach item for a little old lady. I knew these things mattered more than the societal norms by which we usually judge our lives. As Louisa Peck, another near-death survivor explained on the Coming Home podcast: "It is not useful to personify God as some dude in the sky... I can also be a conduit for God... my job is to leave each person I encounter a little happier than they were. And I take this in everything I do... people that I pass on the street..."[36]

Acknowledging her human limitations, Peck knows she can't be a perfect representative of God, yet she strives to live this ideal every day, simply because it is what matters most. "Sometimes I'll be in the airport, and I'll get overwhelmed, and I'll just say to Him, 'I can't smile at everybody!'"

My degrees, my business, my outward achievements didn't matter unless they were helping someone. Being of assistance to others simply had to be a feature of my daily life if I was to live the messages I had gleaned from my metaphysical research. And it was this realisation of what truly matters that enabled me to move through my fears to engage with grief and sadness. In conducting grief therapy, I had to lean into death.

Evenings and weekends became filled with grieving clients as I found fulfilment in uplifting others. It was my new passion. I had a vision to create an online 'virtual private practice' to provide IADC therapy to anywhere in the world. I knew it could help bereaved people in ways traditional therapy could not. It healed them in ways that were surprising and inspiring, yet I was no longer fazed by clients seeing colours and lights, feeling the presence of their loved ones, or crying tears of joy when only moments before they were in deep distress.

But IADC therapy needed more scientific evidence to establish its credibility in the eyes of the broader professional community, and to reach more therapists and their clients. Along with my new friend John Daniels – a kind, inquisitive, and intelligent seventy-something psychologist from Queensland – we saw 43 participants over the course of almost a year in an approved study through the University of Adelaide. More than three quarters of them reported having an ADC. We saw significant reductions in their grief symptoms, average daily sadness, and depression. All but one of the participants said they felt lighter, less sad, or better able to move forward as a result of their two 90-minute sessions. And around two thirds of those who likely met criteria for a diagnosis of Prolonged Grief Disorder before treatment, fell below the diagnostic threshold after their two sessions. Our results also showed you didn't need to have an ADC to benefit from the therapy, and it didn't matter whether you were in-person or on Zoom.

IADC therapy can't reverse the reality of a loved one's death. But it can significantly reduce the sadness of a grieving person and help them to live again in spite of their loss. Studying ADCs and NDEs also taught me that death is natural, inevitable, but is not the end. And as much as we fear the deaths of those we love, we need not fear our own deaths. Through both my research and personal experiences, I've come to see that death is not just an ending, but part of a larger pattern woven into the fabric of existence.

In fact, life is preparing us for death.

We experience losses throughout our lives on this Earth – living metaphors for the transition we all will eventually make. We alternately fear and grieve these losses and are transformed by them.

Take a child losing her first tooth, or the end of a relationship, or even retirement. Whether painful or easy, these changes signal evolution, growing up. A signpost on the pathways to greater maturity and wisdom. These transformations teach us that death is already a part of our nature. These little deaths, the nexus of our vulnerability and strength, are but hurdles along a much broader, longer, expansive journey than we could even conceive at that moment in time. And the fear surrounding these deaths cannot be permanent. Because new life – the next version of ourselves – comes with every change. Likewise, our multidimensional evolution continues beyond our bodily death and contributes to the whole.

While in this physical existence we feel separate. Our awareness is limited in both time and space to the internal thoughts and sensory perceptions of 'us'. But after death we return to the embrace of all-that-is. When we return home, we are connected again, with a distinct awareness of being a part of everything and everyone. We draw soul lessons from our life reviews, but in order to evolve, we require the amnesia of physical incarnations in which we temporarily forget this divine connectedness. We fear death, but it is death that brings us home.

One day during the early phases of our research project, John Daniels sent me links to interviews with philosopher Dr Bedrnardo Kastrup, whose eloquent metaphors resonated deeply. Kastrup says: "We are part of nature. We are something nature is doing… We are a ripple on the lake. You can't take the ripple out of the lake and take it home with you."[37] To me, the lake is God, and our life is a ripple.

The more I strived to live according to the principles of loving intent and assisting others, the more I realised this is where true spirituality lies. It doesn't require meditation, out of body experiences, or connecting with those passed over to be spiritual. It simply takes love, a conscious intention to assist others, and then simply acting out our natural part in the intricate tapestry of the universe. It is our part in the whole, rather than our individual achievements, that matters most. Were others uplifted by you? Were they comforted? Were they left somehow better with your influence than without it?

In this sense, our lives are not really about us. By being of assistance to others, a source of love in the world around us, we are playing our role and fulfilling our highest destiny. The intention to lead a life of service brings true freedom. Then we can have peace in our hearts at the end of this physical life. Dr Kastrup explains that the western materialist worldview, which assumes our lives are all about ourselves, is preposterous:

> "It's like a blossom in my apple tree thinking that its life is about itself and doing its best not to die. Well, if it would get its way, there would be no apples and no apple trees. The whole thing would grind to a halt. You may think that it is psychologically unhealthy to think that your life is not about you, but my personal experience of living this conclusion is that it is liberating. It's a profound liberation. You no longer have to wrestle with a level of responsibility that is unnatural for a human being, a level of control of the dynamics of nature that human beings simply cannot have, and your life becomes one of service... service to nature."

Having a series of prompts and tasks can help us create a life of service, driven by our love of the whole of which we are a part. Like blossoms on the tree of existence, our loving expression of who we are is our sacred fulfilment of God's wish.

When we act out of love, living our lives as best we can, we are playing our role in nature. We are a small part of the entire organism – which is God – but our vibrancy, our spiritual health, makes the whole beautiful, and contributes to the fulfilment of its destiny. The helping of others, the smile, the forgiveness, the loving action of any kind, is our blossoming on the tree of God.

When I reflected on the aftereffects of spiritually transformative experiences – from ADCs to NDEs and many others – I realised they provide lessons that all of us can live by, whether we've had such an experience or not. These lessons reflect our deepest nature, they give us a pathway for spiritual evolution as part of the universal whole and lead the way home. Researchers like Professor Holden and her colleagues have widely reported these aftereffects, some of which I present below. Let's also extract the lessons they provide, sacred clues for living a truly spiritual life:

Aftereffect	Lesson
A decreased fear of death	Do not fear death
A greater appreciation for life	Treat life as sacred
A profound sense of spirituality	We are primarily spiritual beings by nature
A deepened sense of purpose	Your life matters
More empathy and compassion towards others	Other people are part of the one whole, just like you
A renewed sense of responsibility to act ethically and be of assistance	To act with love is to blossom on the tree of God
Material success and external accolades become less important than personal and spiritual growth	Our spiritual growth, not materialism, is what matters when we return home

We don't need to experience death and return, or communicate with a deceased loved one, or have an out of body experience in order to apply these lessons. Our spiritual blossoming as part of the tree of existence comes from expressing our true nature: that we are a part of God.

Here I have compiled a list of questions – spiritual tasks – that may resonate with the instincts of your true nature and help you progress in your own evolution:

- How can I be more loving in my everyday life?
- Given my circumstances and personal gifts, how can I best be of assistance to others?
- Who or what do I most need to forgive in order to move forward?
- What do I need to ask forgiveness for?
- What external or material thing have I prioritised in my life, to the detriment of my close personal relationships?
- What accolade or accomplishment have I hung my hat on but probably means little in the afterlife?
- If this lifetime is for the purpose of spiritual evolution, is there something I have been avoiding that I need to acknowledge and engage with?
- What small things have I paid too little attention to that matter more than I've realised?
- Am I using the strengths nature has given me, to the benefit of the whole?
- Am I fully present and open hearted in my interactions with others?
- Do I fully consider how other people feel when I interact with them?

- Do I notice my automatic judgements, and pause to reconsider them?
- Do I hold love in my heart, as my fundamental intention toward others and the world around me, every day?
- What part of life have I been struggling to control, but I am not ultimately responsible for?
- How can I best express my nature, as a part of God, in a way that will fill me with peace when I die?
- How can I change the way I relate to myself that will best help me accomplish the above?

Asking myself these questions caused a profound positive shift within me. Mundane daily tasks became spiritual missions: being more patient in my parenting of Jasper; holding loving intent and remaining present when talking to Annabel; rising above my own trauma and fear to help others with grief, loss and death.

I hope these questions can help you, too. These tasks make a spiritual life. They are the keys to a life of service. Be inspired by your divine nature and feel the immense relief in surrendering to it. Let love become not only the guiding theme of your life, but the prevailing feeling of your life. You'll feel it in your Day Review, and you'll eventually feel it in your life review.

Opening myself to this universal love, and in deference to the sacred whole of which I am a part, a new prayer arose within me:

Oh God, you and I are one. Let my will be your will.

Expressing our nature as a part of God is to be filled with the light and love of the greater whole of which we are part. How can we not be inspired by that? Such a grand opportunity and such a humbling realisation. As the life of the blossom is about the continual evolution of the tree, our lives here on Earth – physical beings with a multidimensional nature – are also about something much bigger than ourselves: service to the divine whole.

It might be intimidating, at first, to realise this is where life's meaning comes from. But remember, there's no external judgement in the life review, only a self-assessment of how well we expressed our true nature as loving, spiritual beings. We just have to do the best we can with the circumstances nature has given us. Dr Kastrup implores us to take the pressure off our shoulders, to realise that it is "silly" to assume responsibility for the outcome of our lives.

> *"When I understood my life is not about me, has never been, and can never be... and that all I am expected to do from the nature that put me here is to listen to nature and play my role as best as I can. Only then did I become really free. Because I am no longer responsible for the end result. I am no longer responsible for the outcome. I am only responsible for playing my part the absolute best way I can. ... So there is a tremendous sense of release and freedom in a life of service."*

Rather than putting pressure on ourselves to measure up to any given standard, we need simply to listen to our true nature and play our part, however big or small that may be. We are to blossom on the tree of existence. If we do that, we will be filled with the peace of spiritual contentment.

We can have a beautiful death.

Chapter 20

Natalie

I found Natalie friendly and easy to talk to, but I also got the sense she had a strong bullshit detector. As a retired paramedic, she'd seen it all and had a practical, no-nonsense nature in the way she communicated. She was going to tell it like it is, which is exactly what I needed for my research. Not someone who was going to be swayed by any perceived expectations of the therapist, but clearly and directly communicate her experience – whatever that may be.

Natalie described her husband Nathan as "a modern-day MacGyver. He was outdoorsy. Adventurous. He just had this ability to do anything with any item. And he'd love to be out in the bush. He could rig up any kind of camping thing from… you know… ferns and stuff. He was full of beans. And very, very, funny. And he was very protective of me and our son and daughter."

Natalie kept Nathan's photo on her desk where she was sitting for our Zoom call and held it up so I could see it. It was a close up, head-and-shoulders photo of a handsome man with a closely trimmed beard wearing a burgundy t-shirt and a light blue baseball cap. He had a bright, carefree smile, looking relaxed and happy; I imagined he'd been photographed at a social gathering surrounded by good friends. Natalie smiled as she held Nathan's photo up for me, and for a moment they appeared side-by-side on my computer screen. Natalie with her blonde hair and brown-rimmed glasses right next to Nathan smiling in his baseball cap – it was easy to see them as a happy couple.

"A good-looking fella!" I remarked.

"Yeah, a bit of a rooster!" Natalie replied with a grin.

The brightness in Natalie's voice and smile when she spoke about the love of her life belied the dark times she was currently wading through.

"I feel like I'm drowning in it," she said of her grief. "I just can't seem to see the end of it."

I recalled our screening call a couple of months' earlier. Natalie had described her grief as "clinging" to her. While she wasn't actively suicidal, some days she felt as if she didn't want to be alive. She said, "I can feel it under the surface all the time. I can just feel tears all the time. Every minute of every day. They're sitting there now. They're just about here (she motioned across her upper chest). It's like I'm only living with my head, that's basically how it feels. And below, that is all sadness. I'm just trying to keep it under control all the time."

I asked Natalie about their relationship.

"Nathan was always telling me he loved me. We were just two peas in a pod. We had a really, amazingly, good relationship. Which is a large part of why I feel so devastated, because I look out there and see a lot of relationships, and I realise what I've lost."

For all the grief and sadness I encountered in my IADC sessions, what stands out most of all is the love my clients feel for the person they've lost. No matter how intense their distress – and, believe me, it could get *very* intense – the love always appeared stronger. I found it inspiring. The power of love was there before the overwhelming grief, and if I did my job right, strong feelings of love would return as the prevailing emotion my clients felt when they thought of their loved one. The sadness doesn't need to win. Love stories like Natalie and Nathan's spurred me on.

"Sometimes I truly believe we are the same soul," she said.

At the precise moment Natalie said that, she stopped and looked to the side, then looked back to me. "I'm sorry, my fire alarms are about to go off. Sorry." Natalie jumped up from her seat and went to switch the alarm system off.

She returned about a minute later. "Do you know that went off in the middle of the night last night?" she said. "And it went off about 2 months ago at the exact same time… it was 1:38am. And normally, if there's a problem with it, it flashes red. I went around the whole house – none of them were flashing red. There's not a problem with a single one of them." She held up one of the white, circular fire detectors. "I actually stood here last night, and said 'Are you giving me a message?' And now there it is again."

I'd come to realise these little happenings weren't so unusual when doing IADC therapy sessions. I'd seen lights flash on and off; random music start playing out of my iPhone; one lady's computer monitor brightness kept oscillating from full brightness to fully off when she spoke about her deceased daughter, and she wasn't even touching the keyboard – it lit her face like a slow-motion strobe. Thankfully, Natalie took the fire alarm thing in her stride, and we continued our conversation.

I asked if there were any negatives to her relationship with Nathan. The only thing she could come up with was that sometimes he was too attached. He didn't feel the need to branch out and spend time with friends on his own, he was content to always do things together, and sometimes that could be a little smothering. But overwhelmingly, their relationship was defined by a magnetic, loving bond, and a wonderful partnership. They made a great team.

On the day Nathan died, he and Natalie had an "amazing day". They were painting the spare room of their unfinished house, the house Natalie was speaking to me from now, some two and half years later. "It got to about three in the afternoon, and we'd run out of paint."

Natalie was in the local hardware store when Nathan rang. She told him the local store didn't have the right colour paint they needed, but the store in the next town did. Nathan offered to get it. It'd be an excuse to take his vintage sportscar out for a spin and enjoy the beautiful day.

"We had this rule about not pushing the old car too hard," she explained. "It was his pride and joy, to have the car to work on, to drive around, but the restoration wasn't finished. It was quite powerful and there were no airbags. I worried that it wasn't that safe."

Natalie had carried on with her day, getting some things from the shops, when she somehow became aware that *something* had happened.

"I was standing in an aisle in the shop, and I felt this rush of air go through my stomach. It was like something rushed through me, almost like you want to dry wretch or something. I just felt immediately like the universe had changed. I had an instant feeling that something had happened in the world, but I didn't have any concept of what that was.

"It was just this feeling of change... dramatic change. I felt like I might open up the news, and there'd be another 9/11 happening or something. I just felt something had shifted. I dropped what was in my hands when that happened, and I just stood there. I was just looking around going 'Something's not right', you know? And I wandered aimlessly for a few minutes. I didn't pick the items back up. I just kind of wandered around in this aisle going 'I don't know what to do', like something's wrong. And then my phone rang."

Natalie's daughter had called her to tell her there was a police car pulling into their driveway. Nathan hadn't arrived home, and it was getting dark.

"I started to call my husband, and I was ringing and ringing and ringing. It was just ringing out and I was leaving messages for him. And I was texting too. I just dropped everything and ran for my car. I got about two minutes up the road when the police phoned. They said, 'Can you stay where you are? We're coming to get you'. I just knew immediately. The police officer said, 'We'll chat to you when we get there'. I kept saying 'Is he dead? Is he dead?' And the officer just said, 'Yes, he's dead.'"

The strongest piece of sadness for Natalie was simply missing Nathan. His presence. His companionship. His love. As is common in the early stages of the first session, her sadness – which was already intense – began to increase. Tears flowed freely from her eyes as they tracked the blue ball running horizontally across her computer screen. She sobbed quietly throughout the pendulum-like swings from left to right. When Natalie reported heaviness in her chest, I asked what was behind the heaviness.

"Just the finality of it all. The finality of never being able to see him or hear his voice. That's the end and it's so final."

After several sets of eye movement, pushing through a relentless wall of sadness, heaviness and emptiness, I asked what she was noticing about her sadness.

"I guess I feel a bit more of an acceptance. This is just how it is. A little less sting I suppose," she said.

"Let's see what happens to that feeling of acceptance and the sting of the sadness over the next set, okay?" I said. "You're doing great. Keep going. Just let yourself feel it. Follow the blue ball."

When Natalie's sadness increased again, after it had started coming down, I was immediately interested in what was going on in her thoughts.

"My thoughts were 'you're never, ever, gonna see him again,'" she replied.

I wanted Natalie to let go of her internal commentary, and just focus on the emotion.

"What I want us to do for this next set is let yourself feel the emotion that comes from that that thought: 'I'm not going to ever see him again,'" I told her. "Let yourself feel that at the beginning. And then, once the blue ball starts, just let that mental chatter drift away. If you notice thoughts come up, just let them pass through. We just want to stay with the emotion as opposed to the thoughts, okay? The thoughts are fine in the beginning. Let yourself feel the emotion associated with that: I'm not going to see him again. And when you're feeling it, we'll start the blue ball going, but we'll just leave the thoughts behind."

The following set was our turning point. Natalie was able to leave her thoughts behind and just go with the feeling.

"I felt really calm," she reported. "I just felt like a real sudden calmness come over me. And it was like the sadness went," she added.

Very quickly, calm feelings started to emerge and grow with each subsequent set. It was a stark contrast to the intensity of her sadness only minutes before. "I feel this tingling all over my body. All around my head and all down my arms… this light tingling feeling."

"Let's just see what happens to that… just go with that feeling. That nice, tingly, calm feeling," I encouraged. I could see she was relaxing now.

"Not as heavy, but I just felt lighter," she reported after the next set. "My head feels lighter, and I don't know… a little bit like I'm going to lift off, or something! I feel totally calm."

Only a few weeks earlier, Sheena (whose son Chris had died from a drug overdose) had described herself as feeling as if she was being sucked out of her body. Other clients had described sensations of lightness, floating, or as if they were entering a deep meditation. Some said they felt so good they didn't want to open their eyes.

"I just feel very peaceful, and I feel a bit floaty. My whole body feels like it's just relaxed. Almost like it could go to sleep." This was a very good sign.

"We're just going to go with that nice floaty feeling," I instructed. "Just think about Nathan in a general way. Let yourself feel that peaceful feeling and just go with whatever happens."

I was now going into 'sneaking up' mode. Even though it was our first appointment and we'd been processing her sadness using bilateral stimulation for barely thirty minutes, I knew Natalie was entering a receptive state in which she would be likely to have an ADC. The key sign was the strong, peaceful, pleasant sensations that were expanding. But I didn't want to disturb her relaxation by suggesting this was the case. Her expectations of something happening could get in the way of the ADC naturally unfolding.

As it turned out, my instinct was right. An ADC commenced, but not in a way either of us expected.

"There's nothing happening with my eyes closed, but I've got the photo of him sitting behind the computer, and when I was following the ball, I felt like his face was changing... to a different photo." She paused. "That sounds weird, right?"

Natalie looked perplexed but intrigued.

"I don't know if it's just what my eyes were doing, but like his face, the face on the photo looks this way" – she pointed straight ahead – "But every time my eyes went left it felt like his face changed" – she pointed in a different direction – "and became a different photo."

Natalie took a breath, still contemplating what was occurring.

"I still see it now. It's still doing it now."

I began to respond, but she cut me off, her voice rising with a mix of excitement and urgency: "It's still doing it now!" she exclaimed. "It's like that photo... I'm not even looking directly at the photo. And I feel like it's actually flicking through different photos... different pictures come up."

I asked Natalie what feeling went along with the photo changing. In IADC therapy what a client *feels* – and how those emotions are changing – is always the best guide to how well the therapy is progressing.

"The feeling is... a little bit of happiness. Like I just want to smile... I dunno..." A warm smile appeared on Natalie's face as she was speaking. "I feel like it gives me a little bit of excitement."

I asked Natalie if she wanted to do another set. She did.

"I just feel a bit ummm... It's not a happiness. It's just a feeling like... I felt a bit teary, from... there was something... I can't explain it. I don't know whatever that photo is still doing... whatever that is, makes me feel close to him. He's here."

"It feels like it's coming from Nathan?" I clarified.

She furrowed her brow as if examining that idea... as if it would be strange to say yes.

"Yeah."

Natalie's pragmatic nature was kicking in. Could this be real? Was the photo of her husband really changing?

"I'm trying not to talk myself out of it, because I... you know... I know my eyes have been moving, and my brain's going to be doing something."

I could see Natalie was contemplating alternative explanations, while at the same time trying to take in what was happening. "But if I don't look right at the photo, right now, it's still moving. It's still... changing. The faces are changing."

She sat quietly for a few moments, just observing. "I can see different faces of his. It's like different photos. It's freaky. I don't want to look directly at the photo for fear that it stops." Natalie was trying to weigh up this unusual phenomenon. Was it her mind playing tricks on her? Perhaps it was her tired eyes. "I don't know if it's my mind and memories of him... but some of these images I'm seeing aren't even familiar to me... but it's him." She finished the session with a distinctly calmer demeanour.

Bemused, but calm.

When we recommenced the next day, our first task was to check to see how she had been since our session ended the day before, and where her sadness was currently at. She reported feeling "pretty good" but also like she had been "run over by a truck." That's one thing about IADC therapy: it is very demanding of the client and is often exhausting.

"I'm not looking for any miracles... you know I try not to be sceptical. But I didn't finish the session and go 'Right-oh, this is exciting. Something's going to have changed', because I think deep down... I guess I don't feel that the therapy can have such a dramatic effect."

I appreciated Natalie's cautious, critical thinking. She wasn't getting swept up in what had happened. It would be absurd to think a therapy can make a really big difference to intense grief in just two sessions. She was thinking logically and reasonably. I couldn't quite explain to myself how it was possible, either.

Natalie told me she'd been wondering about the changing photo, and if perhaps it was a product of her eyes moving back and forth repeatedly. She'd discussed it with a neighbour, she said, and was wondering what the explanation could be. The neighbour had asked what the rest of the room was doing while the photo was changing.

Natalie told her the rest of the room was perfectly still.

I asked her how sad she felt now, when she allowed herself to feel the piece of sadness we'd been working on yesterday: missing Nathan, his presence, their future plans together.

"I'd say a two or a three out of ten," she replied.

I asked Natalie if that was surprising to her.

"Yeah, it totally surprises me."

It was perfectly reasonable that her pragmatic brain looked for the simplest explanation. Something other than 'This man on Zoom made a blue ball move back and forth and now I feel better'.

"I mean… I'm just sitting here in my own mind thinking that's just because that's this particular minute. I've had my kids here this morning, someone's cooked breakfast. I'm going to see them this afternoon. Today I'm feeling surrounded and supported. So I guess in my mind I think I feel okay today, because it's not the empty day that I normally wake up with, you know?"

She could be right. Today was Mothers' Day. Some nice things were going on. Who knows if the therapy session had anything to do with it? Only time would tell. But I had confidence – based on how she responded the day before, and my experience doing this therapy with dozens of people before – that we'd be able to go even further today. And by the time I followed her up in a month or so, she would have been through enough ordinary days to find out if her daily sadness had significantly reduced. We targeted Natalie's new worst piece of sadness: the loss of her sense of self.

"I used to like myself, you know? It sounds narcissistic but, I don't mean it that way. I actually really liked who I was as a person, and I liked that people were happy around me. Without being big-headed, I know that I can always walk into a room and lift the mood. And I've always been someone people feel happy around. But I'm not that person anymore. I hate that. And no matter how hard I try, I cannot be that person anymore. It's like I've completely lost who I used to be.

"I was someone that used to be invited first to go out to dinner and things. Now I'm the one that's invited last. And I think a large part of where that comes from is not feeling like I belong. A big part of grief is just feeling like you don't belong anywhere. I feel married. Nathan and I had been together since we were teenagers. I've never lived in this life without him. It's just always been the two of us, and I still feel like I'm in a couple. I've never been that person in their thirties, looking for a relationship – you know, dating and stuff like that. So, I've never had to experience what it's like to be the single person amongst couples, and it's horrendous.

"I don't feel like I belong with the single people, going out and joining single activity groups, because I don't feel single. And I don't want to be single. So I don't feel like I belong there either. I'm in some No Man's Land."

Natalie's voice was cracking as she spoke. Her pain seemed so raw. She wasn't just mourning Nathan. She was mourning the loss of her whole life. It was as if one day she was this happy, fulfilled, grateful person, who held so much positive energy she could light up a room, and the next she didn't recognise her life – or herself. She felt lost in a void of disorientation. Not knowing which way was up, or even who she was anymore.

And that was deeply, profoundly, sad.

It took a few sets for Natalie to quieten her thoughts and get into the flow of processing. Intense sadness arose, with plenty of tears. Then things started to move quickly. As usual, after each set of eye movement I would ask her what happened to her sadness. After a few sets she said, "It feels like it's kind of gone. I feel really calm."

With a subsequent set she reported that the calm feeling got stronger. Then…

"The photo is doing the same thing it was doing yesterday."

The changing photo was intriguing to me, but not surprising. In the trove of reading, listening, and watching about ADC-related phenomena, I had heard others talk about changes in photos, including altered images or orbs appearing. ADC phenomena can be incredibly broad and tend to reflect what is most meaningful or accessible for the person experiencing it.

After the next set of eye movement stopped, she was still for a about twenty seconds before opening her eyes. She didn't notice much with her eyes closed, but the photo was changing again.

"I feel that he's trying to show me something," she said.

"Well, there's no rush," I reassured her. "We've got plenty of time, and we'll just see what that message is. Okay?"

The photo started to change rapidly, flashing images that Natalie had never seen.

"I feel like it's a young him… like primary school age or something," she explained.

After another couple of sets it changed again.

"I'm not 100% sure what I'm looking at," Natalie's brow furrowed.

Then, just as suddenly…

"This is his dad," she stated softly; matter-of-factly. "It's his dad," she said again quietly. Natalie nodded gently as she spoke, as if there was a small relief from this recognition.

I asked Natalie to refocus her attention on anything that happens in the thirty seconds or so after she closes her eyes. She was understandably anticipating the changing images in the photo frame, but I didn't want her to miss anything that might come to her in a different way. When Natalie closed her eyes after the blue ball stopped, she sat with her eyes closed for about a minute. Her facial expression was changing. She was emotional.

"I had this feeling of darkness. Not as in evil, just a dark... God, it's hard to describe! My head got really tight and heavy. And I felt this kind of sadness move across me, but it was like..."

She paused before continuing.

"I had colours. There was an orange glow. Then the colours went, and it was just black, and I just felt this sadness come across my head, not my body, just across my head like, 'look!'. He came through my head, or something to show me that... he had a sadness or a darkness or something. I also felt that somewhere in there – without saying the words – Nathan was telling me he loved me."

I wondered if the sadness was related to Nathan's dad. The emotion is always the biggest clue, and this dark sadness that Natalie was struggling to describe came just as Nathan's dad had appeared in the photo.

"There's something about that photo," Natalie was pondering deeply what it all meant. "I feel like I was getting a picture of Nathan when he was younger and then a picture of somebody else. It was a picture of his dad. His dad was very volatile. I disliked him a lot. Nathan hung in there with the relationship, but he gave Nathan no time."

Something important was happening, and I wanted to keep Natalie as relaxed as possible to see if the experience would now deepen or intensify.

"Colours are often a sign of an ADC unfolding. If we go back into that again, stay really relaxed and just let it come to you. I think you're doing great. Just let it come to you. Are you happy for us to do that?"

"Yep," she replied. Natalie was committed to the process. She'd experienced enough, and the changes in her emotions – along with everything she was witnessing in the photo – had convinced her to see this through, no matter how sceptical she may be.

"So... just think about Nathan... and just be open to whatever happens. Follow the blue ball," I instructed.

Nothing happened.

I wondered whether our speculation on what was going on in the photo had activated Natalie's thinking brain too much. IADC therapy always works on the level of feeling, not thinking. I needed to switch her back.

"One of the things that you mentioned to me yesterday was about how Nathan was always a protector," I said. "He was this protective figure protecting you and your son and daughter. And you described an immense amount of love and closeness in your relationship. What I'd like to do now, if it's okay with you, I just want you to let yourself feel that feeling, that sense of being protected, that sense of love, because that was such a part of your connection to Nathan. And I just want you to think about Nathan in a really general way, but feeling that love, that sense of being protected and just go with whatever happens. Is that okay with you?" I asked.

"Yep," she replied.

Just as I'd hoped, the colours returned. She felt calm. We were back on track!

The photo changing was significant and interesting, but I wanted to see if the experience turned into an 'internal' ADC. I wanted Natalie to get the full emotional benefits of strongly feeling a connection to Nathan.

I went straight into another set of eye movement. "Just go with that calm feeling, Natalie. Just see what happens to the orange glow and to the calm feeling. Just stay really relaxed, and just go with whatever happens. Follow the blue ball."

When she eventually opened her eyes, she wiped tears away.

"I almost had to stop looking at the ball to tell you what the photo was doing, because it was becoming a moving face. His mouth was moving like he was saying something. Then, when I closed my eyes, I saw… You know when lava is coming out of a volcano? I saw this orange glow that was getting brighter and brighter. And I just felt this real joy, like this real comfort in it. I can't say I saw him or anything like that, but I felt this real happiness. Like I was somewhere happy. Like something happy had passed through me. It was really nice. I didn't want to open my eyes!"

This was a breakthrough. Natalie had gone from incredible sadness and distress to happy tears.

Although she described the next set as a disappointment compared to the previous one, the photo phenomenon was now ramping up. "The photo changed. That photo's crazy shit. He's showing me somebody. It's somebody else's face. It's a man. With a shorter face. Like a plumper face. Someone that looks bad."

Then, realisation. Nathan's father was appearing in the photo frame again. Her tone became more definite.

"It's his dad. It's very much like a photo of his dad when he was in his twenties and thirties, and he had like a short moustache, and very tight, curly hair, and a little fat, round face. I reckon it's him. I feel like Nathan's showing me that."

Natalie was trying to put the pieces of the puzzle together now. What was it with Nathan's dad appearing?

"I guess there must have been more that he never told me about. His dad could be quite volatile."

I asked Natalie what she made of the experience of the love and orange lava.

"I genuinely felt that he was with me. I felt a real comfort in it. I felt that with that warmth and that feeling of love that went through me… was just for me to know that this was real. I almost wanted to say thank you. It was a message to let me know I was loved."

Later that evening I received an email from Natalie:

Hi Tom

I felt a bit distracted as we finished up this morning and feel that I didn't properly thank you for accepting me into the trial. I do all I can do to heal and feel so grateful that you gave me the opportunity to be a part of this treatment.

As you suggest, I'll stay open minded to whatever happens or changes, but I wanted to let you know that this afternoon I didn't feel exhausted like I did yesterday. I went out with my kids and family for Mothers Day and felt happy and positive. I laughed from a deep place of genuine joy and connection, and felt like I was actually funny for the first time since Nathan died. I made jokes that felt natural and made me laugh, and I got joy from seeing everyone else laughing.

Small steps but maybe big steps? I have hope and I look forward to seeing if it's a lasting and more permanent change.

Early days but I wanted to let you know what this afternoon brought me, simply because it was a very significant change for me in how much happiness I felt just being with my family today.

Thanks again for including me and I hope I'm a success story off the back of your treatment trial.

I hope you had a nice Sunday afternoon Tom.

Kind Regards

Natalie

A month later I emailed Natalie for her 1-month post-treatment questionnaire, and offered her a debrief over Zoom, as I would for all participants in my study. She wrote back a couple of hours later:

Hi Tom
I feel very different! I would love to zoom and talk to you about
the change in me.

When we caught up over the Zoom call, I wasn't quite sure what to expect. But whatever her experience had been, I knew Natalie was going to tell it to me straight.

"Well, a really big change in my sadness... dramatic," she reported. "We did our last session on the Sunday. On the Tuesday I had a really horrendous day. Like, a really horrific day. I was really good on the Sunday, on the Monday I was really good, the Tuesday was horrendous, and then I woke up the next day feeling better and I've been the same ever since.

"I feel like the sadness... I don't want to say it has disappeared because it bubbles away sometimes. But I'm almost struggling to cry."

Natalie told me the reduction in her sadness meant she now had to focus on other aspects of her life, such as finding a new sense of meaning and purpose. She was no longer consumed and distracted by sadness and was experiencing hours at a time without even thinking about Nathan. "And I don't feel any guilt from that. I've really noticed from that Wednesday – and every day since – I now just wake up in the morning and think 'what am I doing today?' rather than waking up and thinking 'Oh God, I'm still alive.'"

Reflecting on the actual ADC with the 'lava', she said: "I have not forgotten it. It was such an amazing feeling. I couldn't stop smiling. I just remember the joy! I felt utter and complete joy. Like someone had filled my body with happiness. God, I didn't want to let it go. It was amazing. And I've got a really clear picture of that orange and gold light. I see that sometimes in my meditations. I have had that feeling again... that I am being wrapped up by him."

"That's the thing that I find remarkable about this therapy," I reflected. "In two lots of ninety minutes we went from such intense sadness, like nine or ten out of ten – in terms of intensity – and then smiling with joy and happiness and feeling filled with love. That still strikes me as completely bizarre, that that happens, and yet it happens a lot."

"It's crazy," she said. "I was really cautious not to force myself to feel that. Because I didn't want to come out of the end of this and go, 'Nothing's changed for you, you're just making yourself feel like it has because you're that desperate to not feel this bad'. I was really cautious to not be too convincing to myself, just to get up every day and see what it feels like.

"I had a couple of friends who I didn't mention it to, until they said, 'You look different'. They can actually see the difference in me. I had a friend last week who messaged me from overseas, who said to me 'Has something changed with you? Because your text messages sound different. You're sending funny messages. You sound like you've come to life again'. So, people are really actively seeing changes in me."

The deep and abiding sense of satisfaction I felt from working with Natalie and others like her justified all the effort I'd invested to date: the late nights, the weekends, the intense logistics of managing a research project around my day job. And most of all, mustering the courage to face sadness, loss, and death, again and again, despite my natural instinct – like most of us – to focus on anything other than death.

Natalie was measured and honest in her assessment, and her assessment confirmed the outcome that I hoped for – and now expected – with each grief client I saw: that sadness no longer defines each day, and they can return to living fully again.

"I would say I am dramatically improved," Natalie said. "It has very much changed me."

Chapter 21

The Little Things Are The Big Things

When I reflected on the amazing changes in Natalie and the other grief clients that John and I saw in our university research, it was clear that several key things were crucial to clients becoming 'unstuck' from their grief during IADC therapy. I now believe that these are also things likely to be broadly helpful for anyone dealing with grief:

Be open to change, and believe change is possible.

It is not necessary to believe in IADC therapy for it to work. But you must be open to the *possibility* that it might work. Those clients who held strong beliefs that "my grief will never change", or "I'll feel this way forever" were in effect directing their emotions to become stuck. It was as if they *became* their grief.

Openness is also crucial to the occurrence of ADCs. When people have an induced ADC and feel the presence of their loved one, my mentor César Valez told me, they are experiencing the opposite of "they're gone". If a client is so stuck in their belief that they're gone, and there is no possibility of feeling their presence, it makes progress harder. Similarly, I needed to at least be open to the possibility I would see / feel / hear from Nanna again to repeatedly perceive her presence. So be open.

Be willing to let go of sadness.

Psychologists will also tell you that in any kind of therapeutic process, and in personal development, openness to change is a prerequisite for change. A willingness to let go applies not just to sadness but also to any other negative state in your life. It might sound strange, that someone would be unwilling to let go of their pain. But from a psychological point of view this is understandable and common. Why? Because change is hard. Stepping into the unfamiliar feels scary. Some grief clients see their sadness as their connection to their loved one and feel guilty if they don't feel sad.

But when the sadness subsides, you return to the essence of that connection, which is love. The love of your connection to your loved one is the diametric opposite of loss, fear, and separation. When the love is felt more strongly than the sadness – even momentarily – ADCs are more likely to occur.

Trust the process of change, and don't judge it.

You don't need to understand how healing and change works for it to work. And you don't need to be sad in order to love and honour the person who died. Many grieving clients worry about what it would mean to not feel sad anymore, or to find joy, laughter, and happiness again. Was it disrespectful to the person they love? Would it mean they didn't miss their loved one as much?

Only when clients were able to separate the intensity of their grief as a measure of their love for the person who died, could they truly let go of those judgments. Living fully again and embracing positive emotions does not lessen the love and respect you hold for the person who passed, nor does it diminish the magnitude of your loss.

Fully feel your emotions but know that your emotions are not you.

Even when your distress is intense, know that it is not permanent.

I've worked with many people who have suffered through years of intense distress and sadness, yet were amazed at how quickly it could reduce when they relaxed into the flow of therapy. Sometimes they would literally refer to themselves as 'a new person' or claim that they had returned to their 'old self'. You are not your sadness. You are not your grief. You are not your trauma and loss.

Hold your attention in the present.

In IADC therapy, we are always interested in how the client feels right *now*. Not how they think they *should* feel given what's happened. Evaluative thinking – estimating how bad or terrible our loss is – is a cognitive process that gets in the way of letting the emotions shift and change with bilateral stimulation. It is tempting to live in the past by replaying things over and over, or project our concerns into the future with predictions and assumptions, which are rarely accurate. Rumination and guilt don't change the past, and worry doesn't change the future.

Resist your urge to avoid.

Sometimes the only way to get past your worst experiences is to go *through* them. IADC therapy is very demanding of clients, but that's also why it's so effective. People in grief spend so much time trying to manage their emotions that when we ask them to go directly into the most intense sadness, it can be scary. However, it is necessary to access the sadness in order to process it. In IADC and in life, avoidance coping tends to maintain problems.

And keep going.

The analogy Dr Botkin used to guide clients to keep going even when their distress was intense, is that of the dark tunnel. If you were driving through a dark tunnel and got scared, you wouldn't stop and get out of the car. You'd put your foot on the gas. This applies more broadly to life in general. If you are experiencing great pain and difficulties, or if you don't like where you are currently at, don't stop there. Keep moving forward no matter what.

Each of these things help us move through sadness to better feel love and other positive feelings such as peace, calm, acceptance, and gratitude. But the ultimate feeling, whether giving, receiving, or experiencing, is always love.

The reason my Nanna had such an impact on me was her capacity to love. IADC therapy works because when you reduce sadness in a bereaved person, they return to feeling the love in that relationship, rather than having the relationship now defined by sadness. Near-death experiencers tell us the success of our lives is determined by how much love we give. And that is not confined to intimate or family relationships. It's our relationship to the whole world around us.

This is best illustrated in the case of a young Persian man, Mohammad[38]. Mohammad was a young child when his family stopped by the side of the road on a long car trip. Many years later, during an NDE, he was surprised to see this scene included in his life review. It showed him that from a spiritual perspective, the actions we assume are insignificant are usually what matter most:

> "There was a river not far from the road and I was asked to go and bring some water in a bucket from that river. I went to fill up the bucket but on my way back, I felt that the bucket was way too heavy for me. I decided to empty some of the water to make the bucket lighter.
>
> "Instead of emptying the water right there, I noticed a tree that was alone by itself in a dry patch of land. I took the effort to go out of my way to that tree and emptied some of the water

at the tree base. I even waited there a few seconds to make sure the water is soaked in the soil and is absorbed.

"In my life review, I received such an applaud and joy for this simple act that it is unbelievable. It was like all the spirits in the Universe were filled with joy from this simple act and were telling me 'We are proud of you'. That simple act seemed to be one of the best things I had ever done in my life! This was strange to me, because I didn't think this little act was a big deal and thought I had done much more important and bigger things. However, it was shown to me that what I had done was extremely valuable because I had done it purely from the heart, with absolutely no expectation for my own gain."

In other words: the little things are the big things. This simple maxim reverberates with spiritual truth. Loving, caring, forgiving, helping, and showing courage aren't our usual measures of success and status. But they are in the spiritual world. They transcend the feeble limits of the measurable, observable, materialist world. They reflect our true nature, and they elevate us. With them, we can rise above fear and sadness.

We are an inseparable part of nature, and our purpose in this physical life is to express our true essence. Just as the apple blossom's purpose is to open to the warmth of the sun and transform into fruit, our deepest nature is to radiate love to the world around us and develop into the fullest expression of ourselves. We are all part of the whole. Everyone we love is part of the whole. And beyond the temporary limits of time and space, we cannot be separated.

This understanding transforms how we live. Every day becomes a spiritual adventure, an opportunity to be a conduit for God. By living a life filled with small acts of love toward others, you are truly living a spiritual life.

So be inspired by the knowledge of how our actions are viewed by the universe. No accolade, no achievement, and no financial reward will ever compare to small acts of love. The decisions you make when nobody is looking, the kindnesses that will never be revealed publicly, are the things that matter most in the eyes of God.

Be comforted by the reality that dying is beautiful and the deep bonds we have for one another do not die with death. And it is possible for the sadness of grief to be overtaken by peacefulness, acceptance, and love.

Everything is recorded, and we see and experience it all again through others' eyes after we die. This is why practising the Day Review, letting go of judgement, and acting with loving intent in all that we do is the true path to Heaven. A life so lived is how our spirit blossoms on the tree that is God – allowing God to experience himself, through us, in this illusion of separateness, until our time comes to return Home.

What have you done with your life?

ACKNOWLEDGEMENTS

I am indebted to the following people who have supported, helped, and inspired me:

My beautiful wife Annabel gave me unwavering love and support. John Daniels was the crucial second therapist in our IADC research project, becoming my partner in crime and bringing boundless enthusiasm and encouragement. Alida Winternheimer helped me develop my writing (although I acknowledge there remains much room for improvement!). My dear friends Corey Rushworth, Dr Simon Wilksch, Adam May and Dr Anna Bouchard have supported my work and life in so many ways over the past twenty plus years – thank you! My spiritual friend Kim McCaul helped keep my writing on track, became a confidant, provided important feedback on the manuscript, and always acted as if the success of this project was inevitable.

My business partner and good friend Nick Lee understood the importance of this work and provided encouragement. Dr Paul Williamson saved the day when I was in over my head with data analysis. Stephen Berkley inspired me with his incredible film *Life with Ghosts* and became a friend. Professor Jan Holden paved the way, scientifically, for my research and encouraged me to put my ideas into action.

My IADC work has also been buoyed by the support and encouragement of César Valdez, Dr Noelle St. Germain-Sehr, Gary

Beaver, Joy Nugent, Dr Liz Keane, Pauline Glamochak, Shyla Mills, Sandra Champlain, Victor & Wendy Zammit, Christopher Hall and all the amazing research participants and grief clients I have worked with.

Thank you also to Mum (Jane Nehmy) and Dad (Phillip Nehmy) for all your love and support.

I've not yet met the amazing Dr Raymond Moody, but his life's work has been an inspiration for me and paved the way for everyone else in the field of near-death studies.

Finally, I am hugely indebted to Dr Allan Botkin, who – with immense courage and determination – gave the gift of IADC therapy to the world. His legacy now has great momentum, reducing immeasurable suffering and helping countless grieving people reclaim their lives.

REFERENCES

Chapter 2 – *An Amazing Therapy*

1. Botkin, A. (2002). Presentation on EMDR and the discovery of IADC. Talk given at the Chicago chapter of the International Association of Near-Death Studies (IANDS), December 2002. *YouTube.* Allan Botkin, Psy.D. Chicago IANDS, November 12, 2005.

Chapter 5 – *After-Death Communication*

2. Streit-Horn, J., Holden, J. M., & Smith, J. E. (2022). Empirically-based best estimates of after-death communication (ADC) phenomena: A systematic review of research. *Journal of Near-Death Studies, 40*(3), 141–176. https://doi.org/10.17514/JNDS-2022-40-3-p141-176
3. Beischel, J. (2019). Spontaneous, Facilitated, Assisted, and Requested After-Death Communication Experiences and their Impact on Grief. *Threshold: Journal of Interdisciplinary Consciousness Studies, 3*(1), 1-32.
4. Guggenheim, B., & Guggenheim, J. (1995). *Hello from Heaven: A New Field of Research-After-Death Communication Confirms That Life and Love Are Eternal.* Bantam Books.

Chapter 7 – *Dying is Beautiful*

5. Moody, R. A. (1975). Life After Life: The Investigation of a Phenomenon—Survival of Bodily Death. HarperOne.

6. Cummings, P. Near-death experience account. Shades of the Afterlife podcast with Sandra Champlain, Episode 162: The Gift of Death.

7. Tolman, V. Near-death experience account. Coming Home YouTube channel. Episode: Tour of the Afterlife: Man Dies and is Shown the Other Side (Near-Death Experience). Retrieved from https://www.youtube.com/live/YJjR8lEbr-A.

8. Brinkley, D., & Perry, P. (1994). Saved by the Light: The True Story of a Man Who Died Twice and the Profound Revelations He Received. Villard Books.

9. Brinkley, D. (2005, December 10). Dannion Brinkley at Chicago IANDS. Presented at the Chicago chapter of the International Association for Near-Death Studies (IANDS). [YouTube video]. Diane Willis. Retrieved from https://www.youtube.com/watch?v=WqLeAhQ9wUs&t=7820s

10. Bolette L. Near-death experience account. Near-Death Experience Research Foundation. Retrieved from https://www.nderf.org/Experiences/1bolette_l_nde.html.

11. Will S. Near-death experience account. Near-Death Experience Research Foundation. Retrieved from https://www.nderf.org/Experiences/1will_s_nde.html.

12. Karen T. Near-death experience account. Near-Death Experience Research Foundation. Retrieved from https://www.nderf.org/Experiences/1karen_t_nde.html.

Chapter 9 – *Reasons to Be Alive*

13. Holden, J. M., Greyson, B., & James, D. (Eds.). (2009). *The Handbook of Near-Death Experiences: Thirty Years of Investigation*. Praeger Publishers.

14. Mäkikomsi, M., Terkamo-Moisio, A., Kaunonen, M., & Aho, A. L. (2024). Consequences of Unexplained Experiences in the Context of Bereavement–Qualitative Analysis. *OMEGA-Journal of Death and Dying*, 88(3), 936-950.

15. Puryear, A. R. (1996). *Stephen Lives: His Life, Suicide, and Afterlife*. Hampton Roads Publishing.

16. Perry, T. (2001). *Dying to Be Alive: Death as Spiritual Healer*. Baywood Publishing.

Chapter 15 – *Science Meets Spirit*

17. Berkley, S. Z. (Director). (2021). *Life with Ghosts* [Documentary]. Jenny Pictures, LLC.

18. Holden, J. M., St. Germain-Sehr, N. R., Reyes, A., Loseu, S., Schmit, M. K., Laird, A., Weintraub, L., St. Germain-Sehr, A. M., Price, E., Blalock, S., Bevly, C., Lankford, C., & Mandalise, J. (2019). Comparative effects of induced after-death communication and traditional counselling on grief. *Grief Matters: The Australian Journal of Grief and Bereavement, 22*(1), 4–9.

19. Greyson, B. (2021). *After: A Doctor Explores What Near-Death Experiences Reveal About Life and Beyond.* St. Martin's Essentials.

20. McDowell, S. Near-death experience investigation. Sean McDowell YouTube channel. Episode: *A Doctor's Fascinating Investigation of Near-Death Experiences (ft. Dr. Michael Sabom).* Retrieved from https://www.youtube.com/watch?v=JKkiPVpbOEc

21. Sabom, M. B. (1998). *Light and Death: One Doctor's Fascinating Account of Near-Death Experiences.* Zondervan.

22. Feurstein, R. Near-death experience account. *The Other Side NDE* YouTube channel. Episode: *Man Dies; Meets His Grandmother And Brother He Never Knew In Heaven (Verifiable Moment).* Retrieved from https://www.youtube.com/watch?v=-DmWsmTFKsk.

23. Van Lommel, P., Van Wees, R., Meyers, V., & Elfferich, I. (2001). Near-death experience in survivors of cardiac arrest: A prospective study in the Netherlands. *The Lancet, 358*(9298), 2039–2045. https://doi.org/10.1016/S0140-6736(01)07100-8

24. Moody, R. A. (1993). *Reunions: Visionary Encounters with Departed Loved Ones.* Villard.

25. Batthyány, A. (2023). *Threshold: terminal lucidity and the border between life and death.* Scribe.

26. Rees, W. D. (1971). The Hallucinations of Widowhood. *British Medical Journal, 4*(5770), 37–41. Retrieved from https://www.bmj.com/content/4/5770/37.

27. Haraldsson, E. (1989). Survey of claimed encounters with the dead. *OMEGA-Journal of Death and Dying, 19*(2), 103-113.

28. Elsaesser, E. (2023). *Spontaneous Contacts with the Deceased: A Large-Scale International Survey Reveals the Circumstances, Lived Experience and Beneficial Impact of After-Death Communications (ADCs)*. Iff Books.

29. Botkin, A.L. (2000). The induction of after-death communications utilizing eye-movement desensitization and reprocessing: A new discovery. *The Journal of Near Death Studies, 18*(3), 181-209. https://digital.library.unt.edu/ark:/67531/metadc798991/

30. Parnell, L. (1996). Eye movement desensitization and reprocessing (EMDR) and spiritual unfolding. *Journal of Transpersonal Psychology, 28*(2), 139–146.

Chapter 17 – *Karma is Now*

31. Ritchie, G. (1978). *Return from Tomorrow*. Chosen Books.

32. Thomas, K. (2022, October 30). *Woman dies; shown the magnitude and impact of thoughts and behavior (NDE)*. Interview featured on *The Other Side NDE* YouTube channel. Retrieved from https://www.youtube.com/watch?v=3j7YqTZkRuE&t=652s

33. Davis, J. J. (2023, April 9). *Most detailed near-death experience ever recorded: Tour of heaven* [Video]. Next Level Soul Podcast. Retrieved from https://www.youtube.com/watch?v=aLhxqy-rLh0&t=1s

34. Rae, C. (2024, June 30). *Woman dies in car wreck; transported to the other side where she faces God* [Video]. The Other Side NDE. Retrieved from https://www.youtube.com/watch?v=-btmpFSY3Q8&t=954s

35. Wittbrodt, P. (2019). *Penny Wittbrodt's jaw-dropping encounter with God after sudden death – Prepare to be astonished!* [Video]. Grief 2 Growth. Retrieved from https://www.youtube.com/watch?v=c8k4tivVj1k

Chapter 19 – *Living an Inspired Life*

36. Peck, L. Near-death experience account. *Coming Home* YouTube channel. Episode: *Alcoholic Dies & Meets her Ancestors on the Other Side (Near-Death Experience)*. Retrieved from https://www.youtube.com/live/l15UGGvFsMA.
37. Kastrup, B. Interview on *The Weekend University*. Episode: *Sacrifice, Meaning, Nietzsche, Consciousness & The Daimon*. Retrieved from https://www.youtube.com/watch?v=9yOs3zfCjvQ.

Chapter 21 – *The Little Things Are The Big Things*

38. Mohammad Z. Near-death experience account. *Near-Death Experience Research Foundation*. Retrieved from https://www.nderf.org/Experiences/1mohammad_z_nde.html.

www.healinggriefwithiadc.com
www.tomnehmy.com

About the Author

Tom Nehmy, PhD, MPsych, has worked as a clinical psychologist for over twenty years. He is also a failed racing driver, former martial artist, and prolific public speaker and trainer. His PhD at Flinders University was based on the development of the Healthy Minds program, preventing the onset of anxiety and depression while also reducing risk for eating disorders (www.healthymindsprogram.com). He was subsequently awarded the 2015 Vice Chancellor's Prize for Doctoral Thesis Excellence. More than 50,000 people have attended Tom's workshops, training programs, invited keynote addresses, and conference presentations worldwide. He maintains an active interest in research and has co-authored multiple scientific peer-reviewed publications. He is also author of the 2019 release *Apples for the Mind: Creating emotional balance, peak performance and lifelong wellbeing,* and his work has been featured widely in the media.

Since learning about IADC therapy, Tom has been on a mission to heal grief. He conducted the research project described in this book as a Visiting Research Fellow in the School of Psychology at the University of Adelaide. He believes the potential for IADC to help grieving people is so great, it is his "moral obligation" to pursue its dissemination. He now provides IADC therapy to clients worldwide via his 'virtual private practice' at www.healinggriefwithiadc.com.

Tom lives with his family in the Adelaide Hills, South Australia.

www.ingramcontent.com/pod-product-compliance
Lightning Source LLC
Chambersburg PA
CBHW030636150426
42811CB00084B/2401/J